AN AFRICAN WIDOW'S
JOURNEY

AN AFRICAN WIDOW'S
JOURNEY

TABITHA MANYINYIRE

Copyright © 2018 by Tabitha Manyinyire.

Library of Congress Control Number:		2018907013
ISBN:	Softcover	978-1-5434-9119-7
	eBook	978-1-5434-9118-0

All rights reserved. No part of this book may be reproduced or transmitted
in any form or by any means, electronic or mechanical, including photocopying,
recording, or by any information storage and retrieval system,
without permission in writing from the copyright owner.

Any resemblance to anyone, living or dead is purely coincidental and not intended
by the author.

Scripture taken from The Holy Bible, King James Version. Public Domain

Print information available on the last page.

Rev. date: 06/25/2018

To order additional copies of this book, contact:
Xlibris
800-056-3182
www.Xlibrispublishing.co.uk
Orders@Xlibrispublishing.co.uk
779376

CONTENTS

(Weeping may endure for a night, but joy comes in the morning (Psalm 30:5)

DEDICATION

In memory of Molly Manyinyire; my wonderful mother, a very humble and kind woman who loved much and cared for all; including loving and caring for her husband's mistresses. The human thread ran through from the top of her head all the way down to the soles of her feet. She taught me that love conquers all; a priceless gift that is surpassed by no other.

ACKNOWLEDGEMENTS

To my obedient children Farai, Fungai and Kudzai; it has not always been easy, but you have dutifully walked this journey with me. To my great friend JHS, I believe it was by Divine appointment that our roads met; I know this is what you do for a living, but I however still believe you were strategically positioned to help transform my life from what it was into what it became; I will always thank God for your life. To my amazing and selfless brother Tim and my adorable sister Ruth; I will always be indebted to you; you have always been there for me, deep down the ragged valleys and high up the mountain peaks.

Last but by no means the least; I would like to acknowledge all the widows out there who not only have to cope with the loss of their beloved husbands but must rise to the occasion and raise their children on their own. May the God of grace wipe away your tears and provide you with peace that surpasses all understanding. Above all, may He also grant you strength, grace and wisdom that will enable you to flourish as you play the dual roles of both mother and father to your children. ***The Lord God Almighty is truly; 'father to the fatherless, a defender of the widows', (Psalm 68:5)***

PREFACE

An African Widow's Journey is based on a true-life story. It is set in Sub-Saharan Africa mid-nineteen nineties. In most communities of this part of the world there is a common belief that sickness and death of one's husband is often caused by acts of witchcraft. The wife is usually the number one suspect. In these communities there is no such thing as ordinary sickness, normal disease progression; (known medically as pathophysiology) and there is no natural death either.

Inspired by the Holy Spirit, An African Widow's Journey distinctly highlights how many a time; in most African communities; the devil often uses the most unfortunate of circumstances in people's day to day lives such as sickness, poverty, and death to bring about chaos, disorder, disharmony and animosity even in the lives of the most stable and solid of families and other relationships.

Thank God for Jesus Christ and His death at the cross, and indeed thank God for the leading of the Holy Spirit; as spirit filled children of God, we are no longer ignorant to any of Satan's devices. Hallelujah!

Faced with a gravely ill husband who inevitably dies within months; the young widow Naomi is left holding nothing except her three small sons; who also soon get removed from her as the society is also paternalistic; effectively leaving her with nothing; at least for a while. She is accused of bewitching her husband and is tormented and abandoned by her once loving and supportive relatives.

Completely lost, speechless and overwhelmed Naomi surrenders everything into God's capable hands right from the very beginning of these unfortunate events and through it all she makes a deliberate, conscious decision that she is not going to utter a single bad word against anyone; neither does she even attempt to defend herself. This would turn out to be the best decision of her entire life as she and her three sons; through God's amazing favour and grace would miraculously and spectacularly rise from the darkest, bottomless pit of contempt, poverty and despair to mountain peaks of unspeakable joy, peace and superabundance in all areas of their lives, much to the amazement of all, including Naomi herself.

This therefore is not a tragic story of an unfortunate African widow's despair and distress. Much to the contrary; this is a delightful testimony of God's amazing kindness and goodness to all those who submit to His authority and who fully entrust Him with all their battles. Battles will always be there! It is a story of how goodness will always prevail over evil because to all those who believe; *"Weeping may endure for a night, but joy comes in the morning"- (Psalm 30:5).* This is real. This is true. This is amazing.

FOREWORD

In this book you will read how many God-breathed Scriptures helped and guided a young African widow, with her three young sons, to walk through the darkest valley of grief and loss with dignity and humility.

As Jesus hung on the cross at Calvary he cried out: "My God, my God, why have you abandoned me?" As he faced his impending death, Jesus recalled the words of the psalmist David, centring his dying thoughts on the God-breathed Scriptures that he had lived his life by.

When I visited Mfuwe, Eastern Zambia in 2014, I remember visiting the home of a young widow whose husband had recently died with kidney failure. Not only was the widow grieving the death of her husband, but she was also having to cope with the loss of her children too. Her husband's family had taken her children away to their home hundreds of miles away. I felt sorrow for the untimely death of her husband but also for the devastation of the loss of her children too.

This true story is full of hope in adversity. Through mentorship of the Holy Spirit, my sister-in-Christ Tabitha has articulately narrated how darkness will always be dispelled and overpowered as God is always there to shine His light even in the darkest of places. As you read this book, maybe facing your bereavement, alone or with others, my hope is that you will gain a deeper understanding in the devastation and painful shock of loss that comes when death crashes into everyday life.

May God give you his insights so that you will be better equipped to travel the roads of loneliness and grief that we will all journey sooner or later. Be inspired! I wish you God's many blessings.

Hilary Buckingham

CHAPTER ONE

ABANDONED BY THE WAY SIDE

We are hard pressed on every side, but not crushed; perplexed, but not in despair; persecuted, but not abandoned; struck down, but not destroyed. (2 Corinthians 4:8-9)

Here I was sitting here in this sweltering room gazing into the damp and mouldy ceiling, wondering. Wondering how I had got here. How had my once so perfect life got to this point? When and how did it all go downhill that quickly? What else could go wrong now?

Well, if my intuition, sixth or common sense; whatever is the correct terminology for it; was still working as it should, what else could possibly not go wrong with my life now, would have been nearer the point. Just then the wall clock mounted high up the wall in front of me chimed. I looked at it and noticed it was exactly 5 o'clock in the evening.

At that precise moment I had an overwhelming feeling that something; something fundamental had irretrievably broken from within me. The feeling one gets when one has been holding and guarding something precious religiously with both hands then the precious ornament slips through the fingers and crushes to irreparable minute pieces on the

1

hard-concrete floor. As bizarre as this may sound; the sense of loss and brokenness felt real and final.

As I continued gazing at the clock, somehow warm tears started pouring down my cheeks involuntarily. I rummaged through my handbag in search of pocket wipes to wipe away the tears before anyone noticed. How bizarre? Fresh tears continued pouring down my face effortlessly nonetheless. At that point I politely asked Grace my hairdresser; to stop plaiting my hair any further. Grace asked if I was alright and tried to explain that she had just braided less than half of the hair on my head. I apologised to Grace and politely requested her to assist me to un-do the plaits that she had already done as I needed to leave as soon as possible. I also reassured Grace that I was going to pay her the full price. I began to un-do some of the plaits myself while Grace who by this time was understandably bewildered began to remove some as well. By the time we finished removing the braids the tears had stopped running.

Grace had been my hairdresser for the past three years. I frequented the Modern Hair Creations Saloon either on Friday late in the afternoon after work or on Saturday morning depending on my weekend events calendar. However today was neither a Friday nor a Saturday; which in itself must have been a bit odd for Grace? Over the years my introvert personality had successfully forbidden me to say very much about my personal life; particularly to people outside family or friends. After un-doing all the braids I put on my head scarf; apologised and at the same time thanked Grace for her time. After making my full payment and tip I left, got into my car and drove straight back home.

As I approached our modest two-bedroom bungalow in Amaveni I saw Chipo's posh red Mercedes Benz parked just outside the gate to my house. Next to it was another car whose owner I did not recognize. Chipo was married to my husband David's brother Robert. Chipo had not just been a sister-in-law to me; being the first born in my own family Chipo was like the big sister that I never had. We were always there for each other. My children were Chipo's children and likewise her children were just like my children. We both had three boys each. We cared deeply about each other; we had a beautiful relationship; yes, until about two months ago when she began to treat me like the great wizard of Oz.

Since my husband David had been diagnosed with a vicious malignant tumour three month back; Chipo and her husband Rob had not visited our house nor made any telephone contact with me at all. Our houses were just a mere fifteen-minute drive from each other. I was also informed through my sick husband that I was now also banned from my relatives' home and the main family homestead in the village. The past two weeks had been particularly difficult as David had been admitted to the local private hospital and we all had to meet by his bedside on numerous occasions.

As per traditional custom David's immediate family had consulted a (n'anga) medicine man or witchdoctor to find out what had brought on the terrible illness and had been told that I was the culprit. The reason given for why I had done this evil thing of inflicting such a deadly disease onto my husband; the father of my three very young sons was; "so that I can become rich from my husband's money after he had died". How the family found this plausible and rational given that David did not have a stash of money put away anywhere nor did he earn more money than I did; has remained an enigma up to this day. In addition to this, it was not a secret that I was the one paying for his top-class private treatment through my work health insurance benefit which covered me, my husband and our three children. How could any of this alleged witchcraft and motivation for doing so make any sense to anyone?

Recommendations and guidance from the consulted witchdoctor were that I was no longer allowed see or be with my husband unsupervised. I was not allowed to take him anything to eat, drink or wear. Touching him was forbidden and I was not permitted to feed him, even the provided hospital food or the food that the family brought. Much to David's distress; Chipo my sister-in-law was now in charge of collecting his pyjamas and under garments from hospital; washing, ironing and bringing them back to the hospital.

I made no attempt at all to protest or break any of my relatives' commandments and the boundaries remained firmly in place despite protests from observant extended family members and friends who found this as both bewildering and upsetting. Through all of this I said nothing and kept my unique type of peace that transcends all understanding.

And yet now here was Chipo waiting for me in my own house. Before the Lord granted me a full measure of 'my unique type of peace'; I used to feel as though a sharp knife had been driven and stuck somewhere within my heart but not deep enough to kill me; I felt mortally wounded by my in- laws' hostility and ill treatment. This was made worse by unending recollections of how over the thirteen years that I have been married to my husband; as a trained nurse, I had always been the first port of call whenever any of my in laws or other members of the extended family members were taken ill.

During these times I had often felt privileged to be in a position where I could be of assistance and had always been available using my knowledge, skills, resources and at times influencing processes at the local hospital where I worked and was highly respected; in order to support and get my husband's relatives the help that they needed with as little hassle as possible. As illness comes to us at any time and in all weather; I had been woken up early hours of the morning in pouring rain on some occasions and had assisted cheerfully. Yes, I had done everything cheerfully and with all my heart. How could people so quickly forget all my good works and sacrifices; just like that? That is where the pain came from.

Just several months ago; before my husband became unwell; I had even cared for and nursed my sister-in-law Chipo in her own home following a difficult miscarriage. It was not an easy task to do as I had to assist her with bathing, washing her soiled under garments and looking after her entire family. I had to leave my own house and children and move into their home for a few days to support and care for her. Of all people how on earth could Chipo shun me and treat me like this? As a married woman herself why could she not feel for me or at least keep a neutral stance just like my sisters'-in-law; David's sisters were doing? These were the questions that kept coming to my mind and when they did they hurt as hell.

However, as I parked my old Datsun Pulsar behind the two flashy cars and walked into the house, I was consumed by a very strange feeling. All the hurting had vanished. This was replaced by just an 'empty space' deep down somewhere within my soul. No pain, no hostility, no anger, no fear. Just tranquillity.

It turned out that the car whose owner I did not recognize belonged to Joel who was married to David's cousin. Chipo and Joel were said to have just arrived ten minutes before my arrival. Before my in laws arrived; in my house were my parents, my siblings, our housemaid and my children. When I walked in my children were playing in their bedroom. My parents and siblings had all arrived at different times and days within the last week after learning that my husband was critically ill; and I was being held responsible for bringing on the illness. For my father the fact that his son-in- law was probably dying became the least of his problems. He made it known to everyone who visited our home that the only reason he had travelled seven hundred kilometres from his work place was for him to come and see for himself the 'torture' that I was being subjected to and to do something about it; if necessary. My father had even tried to ban my mother and my siblings from going to the hospital because he did not want them to meet with and have anything to do with my husband's relatives.

However, my mother being a staunch practising Christian woman of virtue, she was able to persuade my father to soften his heart as "God was going to deal with the whole situation in due season"; she would say.

My father softened his heart; just enough to let my mother and siblings make hospital visits once a day, but not enough for him to make any visits at all. He was so very angry. Because we all knew him well enough; it was just as well he did not want to visit the hospital and meet with my brothers-in-law. He had been seething with anger ever since he arrived and knowing him as we did; it was best he stayed at home.

During his younger days he had been a very well-known 'boxing champ' within the local pubs of every town that we had moved into and lived.

Everyone was sitting in the lounge when I entered the room; they were all silent and each one appeared to be in a reflective mood. The television was switched off. Joel is the only one who greeted me, and I exchanged greetings with him before walking straight ahead into my bedroom. As soon as I entered my bedroom which over the past few months had become more than just a place to sleep and rest for me but also a sanctuary where I escaped to and found refuge and liberation.

I threw my handbag on my bed; pulled my bible from the bedside table and knelt beside my bed. I threw my head on top of my bible and wept quietly for what appeared to have been a lifetime. These days weeping with my bible in my hand had become a form of prayer for me. I did not have to say anything to The Good Lord; He knew everything.

> *For I reckon that the sufferings of this present time are not worthy to be compared with the glory which shall be revealed in us (Romans 8:18)*

CHAPTER TWO

IT NEVER RAINS BUT IT POURS

You keep track of all my sorrows. You have collected all my tears in your bottle. You have recorded each one in your book. (Psalm 56:8)

This Psalm by David to God the Father at a perilous time of his life as Saul pursued him gave me reassurance. On the few occasions that I actually opened the bible and read it the words leapt at me and became alive. My Father in heaven was talking to me on a one to one therapeutic engagement.

"Are you coming Naomi my daughter? People are waiting for you". That was my mother knocking softly on my bedroom door as she was calling me. I stood up, mopped my face dry, put on a warm cardigan and walked out of the bedroom. At this point I felt fairly refreshed and liberated. My body, soul and mind were engulfed by an overwhelming sense of calmness and indescribable peace. As soon as I walked into the living room Joel requested to have my car keys; he explained that following a meeting that they had earlier today; it had been agreed that he would be driving me from henceforth.

For the first time; and with an air of boldness, confidence and defiance that surprised even me I politely told Joel that I was quite capable of driving myself- 'thank you for the offer'. Joel tried to insist, and I heard myself say; "Even if David is dead, I will still be able to drive myself. The first five words fell out of my mouth as if they had a life of their own. Well, why else were these people in my house today after all that had been happening over several weeks now? I quietly and defiantly walked to my car and got in. One of my brothers followed me quietly, opened the passenger door and sat beside me, there was no verbal interaction. I drove off to the hospital where my husband had been admitted for the past two weeks.

Most of my family stayed at home because it was always very difficult for them to get an opportunity to spend even three minutes with David because the visit lasted just one hour and only two visitors were allowed at any given time; David's family and other relatives took precedence and they spent most of the visiting hour as they were from a big and well-known family.

The time was approximately 5.45 pm when I parked my vehicle in the visitors' car park. As we came out of the car my in- laws who had been driving behind me pulled into the car park as well; they parked several cars away from mine. It was almost evening time visiting hour. However, because David was in such poor physical state of health; I was permitted by the ward sister to come in and go as I please; except that my brother-in-law did not permit me to get anywhere nearer my husband without close supervision as I had been declared too dangerous to my husband. Indeed, the boundaries had been set.

Whenever I needed to go and see my husband I had to negotiate with my sister-in-law for a mutually convenient time that we could go to the hospital. Even though David was critically ill and very weak, he had all his senses and intellect intact; he was able to observe what was going on and could see that all was not well with me. This only served to increase his distress and agony. On some occasions he had gestured to me and with a very weak voice asked for me to go close to him and hold his hands, but this was not permitted and, so I kept my distance and pretended that I had not understood. Occasionally I thought I saw his eyes well up with tears and this caused my own tears to well up, but I fought them off vigorously. This was probably one of the hardest things to happen to anyone. It was simply heart breaking.

My in- laws, friends, relatives and everyone in the small community that we lived all knew we had always been inseparable. Even our three sons had always had issues with the level of our closeness as they often complained that we cared about each other more than we cared about them. The father would jokingly tell them that his relationship with 'my girl' as he often affectionately referred to me when he was talking to his children; always came first because 'my girl' got here first before you three boys got here. This would be preceded by play fighting and after this there would be a trip to buy ice cream and potato crisps at the local kiosk by the gas station. David was not just a great husband; he was an amazing hands-on father to his children and was equally loved by his nephews; i.e. his brothers' children.

My youngest son particularly was not happy at all about how his father often appeared to monopolise my attention and affection. I can recall how one evening we had to rush to the local Casualty department (Accident and Emergency service) where we had to manufacture a plausible story of what had happened when my husband sustained a 'black eye' from my almost two-year-old son Gerald who suffered from a severe form of Oedipus complex.

What would always happen is that as soon as Gerald saw his father drive into the yard from work; even if he was playing happily with his brothers, he would immediately abandon playing and run to me. As soon as he gets to where I was he would frantically pull me by the skirt from wherever I am towards the nearest sofa or chair. This included even when I am right in the middle of cooking; standing by the stove. Obviously because of the anxiety and desperation that he often presented with at these times I would quickly switch off the stove and succumb to being dragged to the sofa where I would be instructed to 'sit down mamma'. As soon as I sat on the sofa Gerald would quickly climb onto my lap facing me, stretch and wrap his tiny hands around my body and bury his head on my bosom; and would be so anxious that he could be heard hyperventilating. He would turn his head and glance towards the entrance door from time to time with his eyes wide open checking out his opponent, his father; who would by now be about to walk into the house after parking the car.

David was a bit childish sometimes; he used to find this as both funny and also as a bit of challenge and would be up for the game. He would place his brief case on the table and straight away proceed to un-do the little boys' clutches from me with his big hands and lift him away from my lap, placing him on the sofa furthest away; meanwhile with the boy screaming the house down, wriggling and throwing punches at his father's face throughout. My playful husband would then seat next to me embracing me which would only serve to infuriate the little boy even more who would by then be struggling to climb off the sofa and run back to fight his father away from me. Small as he was he was able to put up a ferocious fight.

On the evening that we spend hours at the hospital waiting for David to be seen by the doctor; the incident occurred almost an hour after the usual altercation. As David sat in front of the television relaxed; reading his daily newspaper, having completely forgotten about their little war; Gerald emerged from our bedroom carrying one of his father's shoe with both hands and before observers could figure out what he was doing with the shoe he approached his father and bashed him on the forehead, close to the right eye with the heal of the shoe. Within minutes the eye was grossly swollen and closed and hence we had to go to Accident and Emergency and explain what had happened.

The story that we ended up manufacturing was that my dear husband had been cycling his bicycle very fast, it broke its chain, he lost control and he hit his forehead against a tree. How on earth could we explain what had actually happened?

Our eldest son Joe who was nine when his father became ill, as soon as he was told that his father might not live and therefore he needed to go and pay him a special visit; possibly for them to see each other for the last time; as advised be the Oncologist; the boy asked why the doctors were not giving his father new organs in order for him to live. When told his father could not have new organs the boy then refused to go and see him point blank and his rationale was; "If he is not going to live, if he is really going to die; I would rather not go to see him at all; there is no point in me going to see him;" and with that statement he ran into his bedroom, banged the door behind him and refused to come out to eat or talk to anyone until the following morning. He emerged the following morning, had a bath, ate his breakfast quietly and went to school using public transport.

Joe and his father had been an apple of each other's eye for about 5 years before the arrival of Jack and Gerald. Since Joe had started primary school their relationship appeared to have become like a roller coaster ride; complete with exhilarating highs and explosive lows. The main drivers around this love/hate relationship appear to have been around homework, punctuality, attention to detail and so on. They both had rigid expectations of one another that should not be breached. Any breaches of such expectations were not received very well by either party.

I remember having to rebuke them one by one, separately of course; out of each other's earshot on one of the occasions when I thought boundaries had definitely been crossed. On this particular day it was the son who appeared very angry with his father for having dropped him off by the school gate outside the school yard. It turned out that all pupils were reminded repeatedly to tell whoever was dropping them to drive right into the school yard and stop at the designated drop off and pick up points. This was for health and safety reasons; it all made a lot of sense.

The boy later told me his father was not 'getting it', as he had given him this message repeatedly but was constantly breaking the rules. However, the verbal exchange did not start well, neither did it end well. As soon as he saw his father step into the house before even greeting him Joe approached him by the door and started; "Daddy if you do not want to drive me right into the school yard where we are supposed to be dropped off I suggest next time you just tell me so that I can make my own transport arrangements". Before I could say 'stop it' to the boy; the father who did not receive this very well responded; "You are spoilt, I drive you to school every day, you are complaining that I dropped you by the gate; by your school gate; just outside your school? Do you know that my father had a car, but I had to walk miles and miles to and from school every day?"

Before the father even finished the statement, the son interrupted with his voice raised; "I am talking to you my father about the issue of you dropping me off at the wrong place this morning, a place that is not allowed for us to be dropped off. I am not talking about you and your father; if you want to talk about how your father did not drive you to school you need to go to the village so you can discuss that directly with him. You cannot talk to me about your issues with your father, but I can talk to you about the issue of you leaving me at a prohibited place and how you got me into trouble at school this morning.

On hearing the last bit then the father remarked that if he wanted to be dropped off at the right place, then he had to get into the car first and wait for him and not the other way around as he always had to wait for him. At this point I had to intervene just before Joe opened his mouth again to say something else to his father because I could see that he still had a lot to say. All I had to do was to look at him sternly and remind him that he was talking to his father; somehow this always did the trick. For some reason he always seemed more receptive to my authority than that of his father.

If they were not squabbling with each other like this; they would be playing chase, chatting, watching cartoons together and laughing like they were equal and greatest friends of the same age. Therefore, his reaction of refusing to go and see his father, "If he was really dying", though rather strange was somewhat consistent with the explosive relationship my son Joe shared with his father.

A lot of the extended family members found this arrangement where I was being monitored and supervised when visiting my ill husband quite appalling and upsetting and would steal little opportunities to reassure me and let me know they were on my side; but what power or authority did they have?

A close male cousin of my husbands' was so enraged the first time that he heard about it and he tried to set up his own boundaries by giving me instructions that I should not inform anybody that I was going to the hospital. He said he wanted to see for himself what they were going to do about it. He went on to vow that if after this anybody did anything else to me he was ready for war.

I expressed my appreciation for his concern but politely and firmly declined to follow his instruction; he did not take this very well but accepted that he could not force me to do what I did not want to do. I had more than enough problems already; I simply did not have the energy or will -power to engage in any fight of any kind, shape or form with anybody.

After locking my car, I walked up the stairs with my brother and left my in- laws waiting for the elevator. By the time that I got to where my husband was on third floor, Chipo and Joel were already waiting by the entrance to the ward with several other relatives. Auntie Theresa; a very close friend and relative of my husband was also there. As soon as she saw me she walked slowly towards me and threw her arms around me and started sobbing quietly and uncontrollably with her head buried in my shoulder.

I embraced Auntie Theresa and started crying with her thereby breaking my own commandment; "Thou shalt not weep or cry in full view of these people". In the last two weeks several hours of my nights were dedicated to weeping and praying when I was in my own space where even my own mother could not see me in this vulnerable position. However today was a different day? With the closeness that auntie Theresa and David shared, how could I not have broken down and cried with her? Each time Auntie Theresa had visited our house since David has been ill, she always cries like this when I escort her to her car after seeing her beloved friend/cousin.

After spending what appeared like three minutes in Auntie Theresa's embrace I walked towards David's private room with my sister-in-law ahead of me. However, the ward sister quickly intercepted us and took us to her office. I used to work with Sister Gladys; the ward sister years ago at the local District Hospital before the notorious and corrupt new hospital Matron well-known for assigning senior positions to her drinking buddies frustrated her out of the system. Sister Gladys offered me and my entourage seats as soon as we entered the office.

I could feel and almost touch Sister Gladys' level of apprehension as she struggled to construct a meaningful ice breaker. Her discomfort was that palpable. Sometimes apprehension can be infectious; it has the habit of infecting and affecting all those within the vicinity in a very remarkable way. Was Sister Gladys about to confirm my worst fears? Something that I had always known in a very mysterious way, deep down in my spirit since that clock struck 5.00 pm as I was in that hairdressing saloon approximately an hour ago?

Before going to the hairdressing saloon; during the lunch time visiting time; David's Consultant physician had met with me and David's brothers. He had reassured us that a referral had just been completed for David to be transferred to the main Oncology centre in the country located about two hundred miles away for radiotherapy and chemotherapy. He had also explained that a special ambulance had been booked and the plan was for us to leave at 5.00 o'clock the following morning. He advised that I could accompany my husband on the ambulance but would need to make my own arrangements of where I would stay.

As I was not sure of where I was going to live I thought I could have my hair plaited as this would be convenient and easy to manage. I had a glimmer of hope that perhaps with radiotherapy and chemotherapy my husband was going to get better and come back home like others do. Yes, even as I sat here in the ward manager's office with all odds appearing to be stacked against me; one thing that I still had left within me was hope; not even my brothers-in-law were going to take that away from me.

It was hope that made me ignore and disregard Chipo's sudden and strange appearance at my house with a relative of my husbands' who had never visited before. It was hope that made me defiant when the gentleman who came with my sister-in-law asked for my car keys and offered to drive me to the hospital. Yes, it was hope that made me dismiss the premonition that I had experienced as I sat in that Hair dressing saloon.

Hope had also enabled me to disregard and dismiss Auntie Theresa's behaviour as something that she had done frequently over the past three months. And of course, Sister Gladys knew me both as both a professional colleague and a ward visitor with a very sick husband; it was likely that she just wanted to have a quick chat with us and offer us some kind of psychological support and reassurance within the private confines of her lavishly furnished comfortable office; except that comfort as I soon discovered was something that emanates from within.

> *I wait for the Lord, my soul doth wait, and in his word do I hope. (Psalms 130:5)*

CHAPTER THREE

WORST FEARS CONFIRMED

When you go through deep waters, I will be with you.
When you go through rivers of difficulty, you will not
drown. When you walk through the fire of oppression,
you will not be burned up; the flames will not consume
you. (Isaiah 43:2)

Despite Sister Gladys' taking her time to get to the bottom of why she had summoned us into her office; in a very strange sort of way I was rather ambivalent; I was not particularly in any hurry to hear what the good Nursing Sister had to say. In fact, the longer that she took the more I did not really want to hear whatever she had to say. I desperately needed to cling on to hope, because hope is all I had left and that is where my strength came from. It was my only anchor; the magic that kept me standing on shifting ground.

As I sat here; I also remembered a statement made by my Clinical Instructor during my first year at the School of Nursing just over ten years ago; "Even when you become a very highly educated and experienced professional nurse, when confronted by a very difficult situation whereby your loved one; for example your child or your spouse becomes severely ill; a lot of you will be rendered useless because the experienced professional nurse will go jumping through the window and

---

16

the ignorant mother or wife/ husband will come walking through the door". As I was lost in thought I was startled back to the present; back to reality by Sister Gladys's voice which seemed to have progressively echoed into the distance before fading away. "My dear, I don't know how to say this to you; I am really sorry your beloved husband passed away an hour ago."

Apart from hearing as if the Sister's voice was echoing from a distance I also began to experience feelings of depersonalisation; that I wasn't real, very strange feelings that I didn't exist. I remember hearing my own voice also making an echo and asking Sister Gladys at what time he had died and if I could go and see him before he is taken away to the funeral parlour. Even the entire environment that I had frequented and known for the last two weeks appeared to have suddenly changed; and I began to feel as if I was floating; floating outside space and time.

Sister Gladys must have walked me to the private room where my dear husband had spent his last few weeks here on earth. As I entered the room there was David appearing to be asleep, now at peace; without any pain or heartache. I stretched out my hand and picked up David's medical records that were at the bottom of his bed. They read in part; 'Stopped breathing and certified dead at 5.00 PM on this day 16th June 1996. Exactly the time that I had felt something break from within my soul as I was in that hairdressing saloon earlier on; what was that strange phenomena? Is this normal? I had never heard anybody talk about this before. So, this is what that very real but truly strange phenomenon meant.

> **For all flesh is as grass, and all the glory of man as the flower of grass. The grass withers, and the flower thereof falleth away. (1 Peter 1: 24)**

Ironically on my deceased husband's bedside were the three 'Happy Father's Day to An Amazing Dad' cards that I had brought in earlier that morning from our three sons. Though evidently in pain and distress, David had marvelled and enjoyed reading every one of them. I had bought the cards the previous week and had given all of them to Joe who after writing his own message on his card had consulted the two younger brothers about what special messages they wanted written on their own cards and had written these on their behalf verbatim.

Was this the cruellest thing to happen to my children? How could these three poor souls lose their father on Father's Day? So, from this day going forward; while every other child celebrates Father's Day with their fathers year after year my three sons will always be reminded of the day their own father was taken away from them? How was this fair?

I picked up all the cards and began to painstakingly read them to myself through blurry eyes full of tears that were now pouring from my eyes like a tape whose valve has stopped working. 'I miss you dad, I want you to come home today, please come back home today. Please daddy. I love you'; this particular message was from Jack. "Daddy, I want you to come and take me to buy ice cream today"; this short message was from Gerald. The last one was from Joe, it was simply written; "You are the best dad in the world, you are my hero, I will always love you. Please get well, I miss you."

Strangely enough, it was at this precise moment that the physical pain; real heartache and the reality of my circumstances kicked in. I was cruelly catapulted back to the real world. As I stood here I felt my heart break and all I could see now was a black shade of pure darkness. My whole world had just turned upside down and there I was hanging by the thread. What was I going to tell my children? They wanted their father back home today? Even more frightening; 'what was I going to tell Jack who had never slept peacefully through a single night since his father left home and was hospitalised almost two weeks ago?

Since his father went into hospital Jack had settled into a rigid uncompromising routine of crying himself to sleep for long periods whenever it was getting dark, from about sunset well into bedtime. He would cry the house down so much so that the neighbours had raised their concerns and now and again could be heard gossiping about it. He would be crying and pleading; 'I just want my daddy here now; I said I just want my daddy back here with me' and would carry on like this intermittently throughout the night and would refuse to be comforted.

There was no respite even when my mother came and was sleeping with him because I still heard him cry from my bedroom every night. How do you reason with a child under the age of four about such a heart-breaking matter?

Of our three sons Jack had a very special bond with his father; owing to the fact that his younger brother came a little too soon, before he was two years old and hence his place on my lap was taken over by his younger brother and naturally his bond with his father was enhanced.

Unlike his two brothers Jack had no issues at all with his father. He adored his father so much so that; over the past year for as long as his father was up and awake waiting to watch his favourite programme, The Road to Wembley, European Cup or any soccer programme that got screened around midnight, Jack was unable to leave his father and go to sleep. His father had therefore developed a habit of pretending that he was going to bed for him to go to bed; however, on Fridays and Saturdays they could both stay awake up to the early hours of the morning.

The only time that he was happy for his father to leave him behind was when he had to go to work; this was after the father had given him a satisfactory reason why he had to go to work, and most importantly, why he had to leave him behind i.e.; "I have to go to work so that I can buy you more toys, ice cream and crisps; and you cannot come with me because there is a mermaid that eats small boys at work". Their bond appeared to have been strengthened even more when Jack came on the scene too soon just after he had just been weaned off the breast. The stronger his bond with his father solidified; the fragile Jack's bond with me his mother became. To him I was just another person who diverted his father's love and attention from him in a very annoying way; not a very nice trait to have!

The last two weeks had been a complete nightmare for us all because of Jack's desire and demands to have his father back home every night. I remember one night the plea was no longer I want my father here, now; but it turned to 'I want to go and see my father, take me to where my father is'; it was particularly dire so much so that the following day my brother attempted to smuggle him through the crowd entrance hall into the ward so that he could see his father; children were strictly forbidden onto the wards.

There were no security cameras, however an alert security guard was able to spot the child and my brother's plan was foiled. In the end he managed to devise a new plan; we parked the vehicle right below the window of the room David was occupying and the poor boy was lifted by his uncle and made to stand on the roof of the car and look up; while I and my sister-in-law were in David's room getting him to kneel on his bed and look out below. As soon as he saw his father's head popping out of the window Jack was so excited and he started shouting; "Daddy, daddy, daddy; I want you to come home today". The excitement did not last very long as David did not have enough strength to keep kneeling on the bed with his head out of the window. I could also see the pain and feel his heartbreak when he saw and heard his son's plea to come home. His fighting spirit appeared to have been slowly leaving him. This was a man who had never been hospitalised not even a single day throughout his life. His visits to the day clinic were very few and all of them had been related to injury; mainly during playing soccer, this was his favourite past time.

Now that David was never ever going to come home; "What was I going to tell Jack"; I must have panicked and appeared confused with this realisation so much so that my constant wailing and desperately asking everyone; "What am I going to tell Jack? How is Jack going to take the news that his father is no more? What am I going to do with Jack;" got interpreted by my in- laws to mean that Jack was my husband's only biological child! How would they have known the challenges that I was going through with this boy given the strained relationships? The more I thought about how I was going to comfort a four-year-old and make him understand and cope with the reality that his father was never going to come back home the more anguish I felt.

Was he now going to cry himself to sleep every night? Until what happens? What was I going to do about this? I hoped against hope that I was just having a very horrible nightmare, but the real pain deep seated within the core of my soul brought home the stark reality of my helpless and hopeless situation. I had no answers to how I was going to cope with this particular child. No one offered any answers either.

It was at this point that it occurred to me that I could not go back home to face any of those children. I simply did not have the courage to go back home. Why should I go back home now anyway? Despite all his love, support, affection and promises; David had ruthlessly abandoned me right in the middle of nowhere with three helpless little boys? How did he expect me to cope? He had always known that I was weak and helpless myself? How was I going to find my way out of this cruel jungle? Why Lord? Why?

> *The mountains and hills may crumble but my love for you will never end. I will keep forever my promise of peace. (Isaiah 54:10)*

CHAPTER FOUR

WHEN THE SPIRIT OF FEAR TAKES HOLD

For God hath not given us a spirit of fear but of power, love and a sound mind (2 Timothy 1:7)

It was half an hour before midnight when I arrived back home. My legs were now aching from all the walking that I had done since slipping out of the little chapel of rest after David's body was taken there at approximately 8 o'clock; i.e. three hours after he passed on. As the chaplain made his way to the pulpit I whispered to Auntie Theresa who was sitting closest to me that I was just going to use the bathroom and she believed and trusted me. I did not wish to have anything to do with the impending proceedings that were due to start anymore. Yes, I did not wish to be part of any of the unfolding events.

As soon as I slipped out of the chapel, I felt very 'light'; I felt as though I was floating as I walked up and down the quiet, dimly lit lonely lanes of the western suburbs; going nowhere; without any aim or agenda other than that I did not have the courage to go home and face my children. As I had been walking for about three hours I eventually got exhausted and sat leaning against a huge Jacaranda tree with my legs outstretched. I made sure I positioned myself away from the glaring lights of vehicles that may pass by. I also kept hoping against hope that I was having a nightmare and that at some point I will wake up to find this is all not true; that this did not happen for real. The more I thought about my husband's untimely death the more intense the pain got; literal physical pain. I felt as if my heart was being shredded with a very sharp red hot gigantic razor blade. Lord why was this happening to me?

"My daughter we have been looking for you all evening. Throughout your husband's illness you have shown us that you are a very strong woman. Do not do this to yourself my daughter; stand up; let's go home. Let us go home to your children; they need you now more than ever before. You now need to be even stronger than you have been, come on; stand up". This was my father kneeling beside me.

"Just as I have been saying to you all along Naomi; even at this very dark time, the good Lord knows best; He still cares about you, believe me"; Standing behind my father was my work colleague, Reverend Ntuli. I must have dozed off as soon as I sat leaning against the huge tree because when I opened my eyes at the sound of my father and his companion's voices my mind though rather heavy, was blank and my body was weary. How else could I have failed to see two huge men approaching even if it was slightly dark?

Many a time in the past few weeks I had found refuge from the torture and trauma of a gravely ill husband complicated by the acrimonious treatment from my brother-in-law in the person of Reverend Ntuli who was affectionately called by the entire community, 'Rev'.

Rev had an amazingly beautiful way of making one see a glimmer of light in total darkness. During the entire struggle Rev lifted high his torch and held my hand as I traversed through the deep slippery slopes of crumbling family dynamics and relationships, steering hard into the unknown future. Rev was always able to make the heavy burden feel lighter and his torch had always shown brightly until today.

23

Today Rev's light appeared to have run out of oil because with every word that came out of his mouth the more irritated from deep within me I became. 'The Lord still cares about you; The Lord has your best interests at heart always?'. Really? Did God really care about me and my children who want their father back home tonight? Why did it not make any sense? What a strange thing to say to anyone? Did God really care about that child who has not had one peaceful night's sleep in two weeks? My wish was that if only Rev would not utter any other word ever again because Rev simply had no idea; he did not know what he was saying. Rev was completely clueless as far as I was concerned.

Here I was, feeling like I, together with my children had been uprooted ruthlessly from the safety of our home and abandoned in a very dodgy remote thick jungle full of dangerous creatures with completely nothing and without protection and my husband had ran off and faded into the horizon and never to return. This is how my situation felt, literally speaking; how could anyone even dare to open his mouth and tell me God wanted the best for me? Was this a very bad joke? Did Rev have any idea at all about what he was talking about or he was just reciting what he had read from the good book; out of context? How could God possibly care about us and at the same time He allows this tenfold tragedy to happen to us? Seriously?

If indeed God really wanted the best for me and my children, then it's either God did not know us that well or it was a case of mistaken identity because what I really wanted most was to have my husband and my life back to where it was. I wanted David to be around so that he can help raise his children. Who was going to do this now? Why did men and women of God have the habit of regurgitating what the bible said without relating their words to people's lived experiences? Surely the terrible dilemma that confronted me could hardly be said to be in anyone's best interests; let alone a poor and weak person like myself.

All these thoughts played in my mind as we headed home on foot. This was before the era of the mobile phone having become a gadget owned by every Tom, Dick and Harry.

Apparently before David's body was removed from the hospital and taken to the parlour, my brother Ken had taken the car keys from me as he had to go home to collect the Funeral Policy documents as they were now needed for the completion of the initial paperwork. I had handed to my brother the entire handbag where the keys were located as it is always a mammoth task to find car keys in my handbag on the best of days. My brother must have rightly concluded that on this day and at this time my handbag was better off without me. Consequently, he had not returned my bag to me and hence even as I was found under the Jacaranda tree, I had nothing with me.

I also kept wondering how my father and Rev could have found me in this dark secluded place, miles away from the chapel of rest where I had sneaked from when people were waiting for the initial church service to be conducted. I only learnt weeks later when Rev confessed what had actually happened. He explained that he and my father had spotted me leaving the room heading towards the bathrooms. When I did not return to my seat in reasonable time they both came out just in time to spot a figure that they figured out was me turning into a side road down the Main street. With time they were able to figure out it was definitely me and instead of walking fast enough to catch up with me they decided they were going to give me space and as much time as needed to be on my own; he said they had shadowed me ensuring that I was safe for the entire duration. How was it that these two men had followed me for hours without me knowing? Well, were any of my senses working at all for me to have seen, heard or suspected anything? Highly unlikely.

As we arrived at home I could see that there was a huge crowd of people weeping and as I entered the house the weeping gathered momentum.

Our friends, work colleagues, relatives, neighbours and some people I did not even recognize were all here tonight sharing in my grief.

Just before I entered the house I could also hear angry voices of some of David's extended family members protesting and demanding to know why they were being asked to leave and go to David's brother's house instead. "Go tell them we are not coming there; the deceased lived in this house and his family is here"; that was David's cousin speaking. However, at this point none of this bickering was of any concern to me at all. Truly speaking I was not bothered at all by where the funeral wake was going to take place. The only thing that gripped my mind and bothered me to death was the prospect of seeing my children; particularly Jack.

All the furniture had been removed from our modest living room and people, mostly women were sitting on blankets spread on the floor. My mother who was sitting at the far end of the room with her back leaning against the wall raised her hand and beckoned me to go and sit beside her as she and other women created space for me. The wailing was growing louder with others also raising their voices singing the commonest church hymn- "We shall meet again in heaven, by God's grace and through having faith in Jesus Christ".

Meanwhile, my mind remained completely preoccupied with the prospect of seeing my children; wondering and worrying about what I was going to say to them. As the singing and wailing grew even louder and louder I then noticed my bedroom door; located right opposite to where I was sitting getting opened slowly but surely; and within a few more seconds my heart sank, and I held my breath; this was the moment I had dreaded all evening; this was precisely the reason I had attempted to go missing for as long as possible so that I can delay this dreadful moment for as long as possible.

There in the door way was Jack standing rubbing both of his eyes with the base of both his palms; in between rubbing his eyes he also intermittently peered through the crowded room, obviously trying to locate where I was. As other women pointed him in my direction I also raised my hand and gestured him to come over to mamma. As soon as he saw me he started jumping over people's out-stretched legs, so he could get to where I and his grandmother were sitting. Other people lifted him as he passed through, but others attempted to do the same but failed as he was a rather obese child just about to turn four. He eventually got to where I was sitting with my legs also out stretched and he sat on my lap facing me with his tiny legs astride and his small arms wrapped around my body. As soon as he was sitting comfortably he lifted up his little face towards mine; looked me in the eyes and said with the softest and calmest voice that has never left me to this day; "Has my daddy died mamma?" Completely flabbergasted I replied candidly with an astonishing level of boldness; "Yes Jack my son, your daddy has died".

As soon as I answered his very precise question I felt his cuddle become a lot tighter; still looking me in the eye he startled me even further by whispering to me; "It doesn't matter mamma, we will be alright on our own" and with that he made himself more comfortable by burying his head in my chest.

As soon as my once troubled son gave me the reassurance that I had needed most all day; 'It doesn't matter mamma, we are going to be fine on our own'; I was completely consumed by an overwhelming sense of peace and comfort that defies all understanding. What just happened in that moment changed everything forever because in that dreadful moment I touched and tasted the goodness of God Almighty. What had just happened was beyond anything that I could have ever thought, dreamt or imagined; it was beyond my wildest dream or imagination. God had just turned up at my direst moment; at my point of need. This was a miracle to me. Hallelujah.

Of course, nobody else, perhaps apart from my mother; had any idea of what had just happened. Only I knew beyond reasonable doubt that

God had just turned up and manifested His presence in that house through a one-minute conversation with my almost four-year-old son; my once troubled and tormented son! Now that I had living evidence that my God still cared and was right here with me; I had nothing to be afraid of anymore.

As soon as my little boy said those reassuring words he soon fell asleep on my lap and my mother took him to his bed to sleep. For the first time in two weeks my son slept peacefully, without crying for his father, throughout the night not just on this particular night but also on the rest of the days that came! For the first time in a while I felt as though the heavy load that I had been carrying had just been reduced by half. This was just so amazing. Not even Rev was able to for-see this would happen. All that time I cried and pleaded 'What am I going to tell my children; how was I going to console Jack and stop him from crying for his dad?'. Nobody seemed to have an answer for me. "God wants the best for you"; like Rev said did not seem to answer my question and; yet it did! God in His infinity wisdom and grace; turned up Himself, spoke and comforted me through the same troubled child. His thoughts and ways are higher than our thoughts and ways!

> *And God will wipe away every tear from their eyes; there shall be no more death, nor sorrow, no crying. There shall be no more pain, for the former things have passed away. (Revelation 21:4)*

CHAPTER FIVE

GROWING IN FAITH AND WISDOM

Trust in the Lord with all your heart; and lean not on your own understanding (Proverbs 3:5)

My journey of faith led me to total freedom from fear. The fact that my son never woke up to cry at all that night and the peace that he radiated for the first time in two weeks was further evidence and a clear indication to me that a bigger force had come into play. This could only be God.

It was then that I said to God I was relinquishing all my responsibilities and cares into His hands from henceforth. I made up my mind that since He had taken care of my greatest fear; I no longer had any reason to worry about anything else that was happening around me. I also made a conscious decision that it was no longer necessary for me to think or worry about what was going to happen to me or my children; nor was it my responsibility to try and put together fragments of my shattered life.

Even though I cared, however I strongly felt that it was no longer in my best interests or strength to take care of anything or anybody. I had tried caring for everybody and worrying about everything during my married life; where did it all get me? What I did now know without a shadow of doubt was that God was able to take care of my worst fears and troubles and that his timing was perfect. No matter what we may be going through he is always right there with us and will manifest at a crucial moment if the situation is dire enough to warrant his manifestation.

The next two days were packed with family meetings; burial arrangements and putting together of David's few personal possessions that he had acquired while he was here on earth. Yes; when it is all said and done nothing matters any more apart from what we have done in order to prepare ourselves for resurrection with the Saints on the day the trumpet is going to sound ushering us all believers into eternity.

My in-law's hostility towards me and my immediate family members appeared to have been neutralised somewhat by extended family members and friends who thankfully were still able to hold on to an objective view of who I really was. Some highly regarded family friends had threatened to walk away from the proceedings and the burial ceremony in protest of the ill treatment that I was receiving; I heard this a few days after the burial and was deeply touched.

As I went through the motions of doing what I had to do in preparation for the burial of my husband I also kept a watchful eye on how my three little boys were fairing; particularly my two older boys Joe and Jack who were old enough to know what was going on. I was humbled even further by God's amazing grace as even Jack maintained an astonishing level of calmness and composure right through to the end. It was simply amazing.

On the third day we all travelled to David's main homestead in the village where his parents lived in a big beautiful newly built house that David and I had made our little contribution to its construction and furnishing. My barring order to this home was briefly lifted for the purpose of my husband's burial; especially that the entire village was now aware of what was going on and people were watching with a critical eye.

> *For I know the plans I have for you, declares the Lord, plans for welfare and not for evil, to give you a future and a hope. (Jeremiah 29:11)*

I am not sure for how long I had been sitting here. On my right-hand side there was David's coffin. Sitting next to me on my left was my God given sister Ruth. She lived so far away, some 600km away; when had she arrived? She appeared preoccupied and completely lost in her own thoughts. She had her eyes firmly fixed somewhere right ahead of her; miles away beyond the thick walls of this house. We did not establish any eye contact.

The massive lounge was filled to maximum capacity with close to a hundred people; mostly women; all packed very close together like sardines. I had known some of these people, but I had no idea who the majority of them were? I simply could not recognize most of them despite having been a frequent visitor to this home and the village for many years; until three months ago when the barring restriction was put in place.

As I sat here I was yet again consumed by feelings that I did not exist; that I was not there. To be exact; I felt as if I was just floating and hovering above this situation; that I was not a part of this gathering or the traumatic events that had brought this crowd together. Therefore; whatever was happening or going on had no ability to touch, affect or hurt me. I felt completely detached and immune to the expected emotional trauma this prevailing tragedy should have presented. As I kept drifting in and out of reality and awareness of my surroundings I thought I saw an elderly lady who was at the far end of the room crawling over people's outstretched legs as everyone was sitting on the floor. She appeared to have been trying to get to somewhere; somewhere urgently.

The strange phenomenon of feeling like an uninterested observer who is watching a battle taking place on the ground from a few hundred feet above the ground persisted. This extraordinary experience gave me the privilege to feel completely de-sensitized from the heartache, pain, thoughts or emotions. I was wholly and truly completely overwhelmed by peace of a superior kind; I had never felt this quality of peace before. Yes; it was the peace and comfort that defies belief in a very literal way; the one that transcends all understanding.

"Muroora; Muroora; (Daughter in law; daughter-in-law); she whispered into my ear as she nudged me vigorously trying to get my full attention. It was the elderly lady who I had observed crawling trying to get to somewhere a little earlier. I did not recognize her at all. So, she had been trying to get over to me after all.

It was the nudge that brought me back from my world of peace and comfort to this real, brutal world of pain and suffering. I gave the wonderful woman my full attention. She then whispered into my ear; "You look too calm and relaxed my daughter; too calm and comfortable for a young woman who has just lost her husband. If you keep carrying on like this the people here will not think good thoughts about you; at least you should try and at least pretend that you are tormented by shedding a few tears; or better still you------;" before she finished dishing out her advice I heard myself responding; 'Thank you very much for your concern grandma; the people sitting here are free to have any thoughts that they may wish; I do not care very much about people's thoughts towards me; I only care about how God sees me; and what thoughts God have towards me'.

Thankfully the dear lady did not take offense; she shook my hand and nodded her head before crawling back to where she had come from without saying another word. I must have drifted back into my own world of freedom, peace and tranquillity as soon as I was left alone.

During my brief interaction with 'grandma' I had observed that even though she had whispered into my ear her concerns regarding my falling short and poor performance at moaning for my deceased husband; I think I must have spoken back to her in my usual calm but normal tone and volume. It appeared as soon as I started talking most people within the vicinity stopped their hushed one-to-one conversations and paid full attention to what I had to say in my defence. I however felt at no point that I needed to defend myself or my actions or lack of it from anyone. There was no point. Everything that had happened to me and was still happening to me made no sense whatsoever. David's death was meaningless. All the things and promises that he had made to me had all gone; blown away by the wind just like an insignificant small dry leaf that falls off a tree and is blown away- to never return. How meaningless indeed.

> *As for man, his days are as grass, as a flower of the field, so he flourisheth. For the wind passeth over it, and it is gone; and the place thereof shall know it no more. (Psalm 103: 15-16)*

David was buried on day four after his death. From my now familiar surroundings; high up within the comfort of the outer space where I continued to float well above reality I was able to see my kids and observe how they were carrying on. In this family children were allowed to take part in all funeral activities. At this point I soon realized that I had been more privileged and blessed than my children. I had never lost anyone through death who was closely related to me throughout my childhood. My children were really unfortunate. Very sad.

I observed that my eldest son Joe was hanging around in a group with his cousins; they were all not very different in age. Joe had his hands in his pockets; a usual sign that he was doing reasonably well. My middle boy was in his paternal grandmother's arms and he was carrying a single white rose. They seemed to have been having a little argument. Shortly I saw my mother-in-law summoning the undertaker and speaking to him. The undertaker then opened the casket and I saw Jack going closer and placing the white rose in the casket and he kissed his father on the forehead before the casket was closed and laid down.

I later learnt that Jack had been arguing with his grandmother and had insisted that he wanted to give his father the white rose in his hand; he did not want to throw the red rose on top of the coffin 'because my father will not know the rose was from me'; he had insisted and reasoned. My mother-in-law had always been more than a mother to me; she was also my best friend.

My youngest son was being looked after by my mother throughout the proceedings. He was too young to understand what was going on.

After the burial the final family meeting was held but I was not invited; none of my family members were invited. However, my God given sister Ruth who had now become my guardian angel gate crushed into the meeting uninvited and informed the quorum that the only reason that she was in this meeting was to get a better understanding of where I and my three children stood in this family at the current stage.

The position that we stood; as Ruth learnt was sinking ground. For this reason, Ruth decided it was time that me and my family and children had to leave even before the final traditional ceremony that is normally held first thing the following morning after someone has been buried. A truly sad ending to a very sad story about a once upon a time a very happy and united family that appeared to live a very happy and normal life full of laughter and was the envy of the entire local community. All that now completely torn down mercilessly to rubble by cancer and death with powers of darkness taking full charge of events.

> *Be sober; be vigilant, because your adversary the devil, as a roaring lion, walketh about, seeking whom he may devour. (1 Peter 5:8)*

As I began the uphill struggle of trying to pick up the bits and pieces of my broken life soon after the burial of my husband, I was convinced that with all that had been said and done; all that had happened, there was nothing that could happen now that could possibly be worse than what I had already gone through. Little did I know!

Under normal circumstances; in a normal world the bereaved young widow is comforted, pampered and protected by her in- laws. She is protected from anything that may worsen the grieving process. This wasn't so for this particular widow. The following six months saw me get to hell and back on several occasions. Due to word going around that the house might be taken from us I had to move from the little house that we had lived in and had called home for many years while my husband walked on earth. Previously I had been asked to take my husband's car to my brother-in-law's house and I had dutifully done so. I was accompanied by a friend of my late husband and his wife. In his infinite mercy and wisdom God had just given me a new and better job seven month before my husband's passing on. My new employer had magnificent staff housing and as soon as I shared my problems with my line manager that I no longer felt safe at home, my problem was sorted.

My line manager supported me not just with being given the biggest house available; I was also supported with a massive removals truck and four big men; all company resources to help move all my property into our new home that was located on the massive grounds of my work place. This was almost ten miles away from town where my brother-in-law and his family lived.

Thankfully my young brother who had just graduated from university and my mother were also still around. My father had gone back to his work place soon after the burial and had instructed my mother to stay around and look after me and the boys for as long as she wanted. My brother decided to stay behind as well as he was extremely close to the boys, especially my eldest boy.

While most new things are almost always associated with that which is desirable, commendable and ideal; there was nothing desirable, commendable or ideal about our new situation. Losing a spouse and moving to a new house are said to rank very highly on life's hierarchy of stressors; my mother and brother's presence was God-send as this helped us a lot to settle into our new life and routine with fewer bruises than we would have suffered.

While living in our nicer bigger house away from my tormentor was probably the best thing that happened to us during this time; it however came with challenges of its own. My poor children had just lost a terrific father; including the benefits that come with having a very loving, kind, caring hands- on father. They had also just lost a place that they had called home for a significant part of their lives and with that loss came the loss of their friends; friendships that they had cultivated and nurtured throughout their short lives in the close-knit neighbourhood where everybody cared for the person next door. Then there was the big question of the boys' education? Yes, it never rains but it pours. Our new life appeared really dark; and it got a lot darker with each new day; especially a few days after we had vacated our house; at the precise moment that my brother-in-law learnt that we had moved to a new house.

I was just about to leave the office after another dreary day at work when switch board placed a phone call through. As soon as I picked up the receiver and answered 'Hello---'; I was hit by a torrent of vitriol and had no chance to say a word, I could not put down the receiver either because I must have been so shocked and terrified at the same time by what was being said to me. My brother-in-law was at the other end of the line. This phone call lasted about thirty minutes, but it appeared I had been listening to this torrent of abuse for a lifetime.

Throughout the half an hour I was not given an opportunity to say anything; neither was I asked any specific question; which was just as well because I really did not have anything to say. How could I have had anything to say when my brain had just gone numb and stopped functioning the very first minute when for the first time in my entire life someone had actually addressed me and called me derogatory names. The content of the speech and the language used was something that completely knocked me over. In addition to that; in this culture for a brother-in-law to address his older brother's wife by her first name was never heard of. My brother-in-law had never addressed me by my first name before.

During the course of this phone call I was called names; I was insulted for thinking that I was clever by moving away with David's children without informing him; I was accused of all sorts. The fact that this was a paternalistic society did not help. Children belong to the husband and his family; the mothers who carry the pregnancy for nine months are lesser relatives than one's father and his relatives; really weird ideology. Towards the end of this abusive phone call I was told that my children were going to be removed from my custody so that they are not going to call 'your future husband daddy'; he said. He said he was going to prevent this from happening with immediate effect. He made sure he also pointed out the fact that I did not have any children when I joined their family and how it was only right that I was leaving this family without any children!

After this relentless verbal abuse and character assassination I was finally ordered to get the children and their belongings ready as soon as possible because as soon as he put the phone down he was getting into the car and coming to collect, "my children"; he said. He reiterated they were now his children now that his brother was no more.

Just when I thought I had heard it all; when I thought the worst was over. Here I was again. In those few minutes I felt as though I had just leapt through space and time and had crossed over into another dimension; deep down an unforgiving abyss. How was I going to come out of this?

Blessed is the man that endureth temptation; for when he is tried, he shall receive the crown of life, which the Lord hath promised to them that love him. (James 1:12)

CHAPTER SIX

FAMILY LIFE IN CRISIS

Know therefore that The Lord Thy God, He is God, The Faithful God, which keepeth covenant and mercy with them that love Him and keep His commandments to thousand generations: (Deuteronomy 7:9)

Suddenly someone tapped me gently on the shoulder and as I lifted my heavy pounding head from the table, my watery eyes came face to face with my pillar of support; Reverend Ntuli. I never heard or saw him enter the room. As soon as I placed the receiver of my phone on the hook, after the very loud clunk, I felt all energy drain away from my limbs; I felt so weak that I simply crossed my arms on the table and used them as a pillow with which to support my head which was now heavy and aching like mad. As soon as I established eye contact with Rev; tears started streaming down my face unabated. Rev just pulled a chair and sat quietly beside me. He did not say a word or attempt to stop me from crying. All he did was pull out a box of tissue that was at the other end of my table and offered these to me.

As soon as all the hyperventilation stopped Rev simply remarked in a very calm voice; "What has he done now; your brother-in-law?" I narrated to Rev Ntuli the whole story about my most recent phone call from my brother-in-law. As soon as he heard about the new challenge of having my children removed from me Reverend offered to come to my house with me so that he could meet with my brother-in-law and speak with him man to man and also as a man of God. Before we left my office, Reverend offered a powerful heartfelt prayer for the Lord to intervene and that his will be done.

Since my brother-in-law lived just about ten miles away from me; it would not take him that long to get to my house if indeed he left as soon as he put the phone down like he had said. We walked home using the foot path as this was the shortest route home. As soon as we were about to get to the gate into my yard my brother-in-law also arrived. I walked straight into the house to give my mother and brother a heads up while Rev went straight to my brother-in-law's car. From the window I could see my brother-in-law coming out of the car and shaking hands with Rev. Thereafter I saw my brother-in-law open the passenger side door for Reverend and he also got into the car. They must have talked for about forty-five minutes before they both came and knocked at the door.

Meanwhile my two innocent younger children were so excited to see their uncle whom they had not seen since the day their father was buried. However, the same could not be said for my older boy, Joe. As soon as he saw his uncle's vehicle pull up he abandoned watching his favourite programme Knight Rider and disappeared, straight to his bedroom where he firmly shut his door behind him.

As Rev led the way into the lounge; they were welcomed by my mother who I had briefed about the purpose of her in-law's visit as soon as I entered the house. This had upset her very much but just for a brief moment. She was a woman of great faith who believed God was in control all the time; 'God never loses control, never; because even the bad things that happen to us; they will always work together for our good in the end'; she had reassured me on many occasions, including today.

Both men were offered seats and greetings were exchanged in a calculated manner. I could over-hear the awkward conversations from my bedroom as I had left my door slightly ajar for this purpose. It was great that the three of them knew each other very well; there was no need for introductions. They had all met and mingled before and soon after David's death. Everyone was aware of the strained relationships and hence the tension in the atmosphere was quite palpable.

However, when my brother-in-law finally got to speak about the purpose of his visit; I was completely gobsmacked and wondering whether I was hearing properly; or I was losing my mind. Given my experience of the past two hours during that telephone call; how could I have been hearing and understanding this well? If indeed my mind was processing this information well, then this was a miracle. It was like a tornado had just come and swept everything away and behind it something new and fresh had just emerged. As he was speaking to my mother; my brother-in-law had somehow; and suddenly turned back into the nice, courteous and caring man that I had always known him to be for all the years that I had known him; until that day when my husband was declared mortally ill.

I overheard him courteously thank my mother for looking after 'her grandchildren'; he was clapping his hands as he spoke as per traditional custom when a man is talking to an older woman whom he highly respects. He went on to explain politely how it would be a good thing for the three children to remain at their current schools, which were located closer to his house. He said he had therefore come to collect them so that they can stay closer to their schools so that they are not stressed by a long commute to school which may affect their wellbeing and performance in class.

He also talked about how he would be bringing them back on Friday evenings and collecting them on Sunday evenings 'so that they can spend all weekends and school holidays with their mother! 'As the conversations in the lounge carried on, I quietly pulled and closed the door very gently before kneeling beside my bed and sobbing tears of relief as I gave some thanks offering to the Lord in the form of prayer for coming to my rescue yet again; with a torch that shed some light on my path at another very dark hour.

However, of the three boys he was only able to take the two smaller boys. Yes, it is true that little children see or hear no evil. The reason why in Matthew 18 verse 3 Jesus said; *'Truly I tell you, unless you change and become like little children, you will not enter the Kingdom of heaven.'*

My eldest son could neither be convinced, encouraged or bullied into going anywhere. My mother and Reverend Ntuli took turns to go to his bedroom to have a heart to heart conversation with him. They both tried their best at highlighting to him how going with his uncle would be better for him; during school days he would be living nearer his school, besides his uncle had several cars and drivers; he would always be driven to and from school every day. This was also to his benefit as he would no longer have to wake up too early in the morning; around 5 o'clock in the morning to walk the mile journey to go and catch public commuter minibuses. He also had to change buses in town for him to get the minibuses to his school as it was at the other side of town. School started at seven-thirty in the morning and hence his commute had to start very early in the morning. Anyone who arrived late at school received punishment; usually in the form of cleaning toilets.

Despite these elaborate pros and cons my son was adamant that he was not going anywhere that is not home. When asked what his understanding of home was he emphatically and boldly replied; "Home is where my mamma is"; before entering into his blankets and covering himself from head to toe under the blankets; something that he did often to express his defiance. This was also, his usual sign to indicate that there were no negotiations or compromising to be considered.

He also completely refused to come out to at least just greet his uncle. It was a huge blessing that we had a peacekeeper present in the form of Reverend Ntuli. Rev was able to speak to the boy's uncle in a constructive way that enabled the uncle to understand the situation in a positive manner. He thanked the uncle for his gesture and concluded by saying of the eldest boy; "If your only concern is the boy's welfare and his best interests; then leaving him behind with his mother is the right thing to do". He took this on board well.

As soon as the two pre-school boys learnt that their uncle would be driving them up and down to and from their Early Learning Centre and bringing them home on Fridays; they were up for the adventure! What also helped was the small age gap they shared; this made their relationship very close so much so that they behaved as if; as long as they were in each other's company they were invincible, they could conquer the world. That they could be left anywhere and survive. They were inseparable. Despite the usual sibling rivalry which was as strong as their bond and love for each other; they were generally a great team, a solid duo, particularly since their father passed away and Jack had lost his preferred friend.

The huge gap between them and their older brother in those early years meant it was always them versus him. As the bigger boy Joe had his own bedroom and, on his door, there was a sign in red bold letters: NO UNDER TENS ALLOWED BEYOND THIS SIGN! Below the wording there was a danger warning sign in the form of a skull with horns! He often referred to his young brothers as 'the terrible twins', particularly when he was talking to me or anyone close. Strangely enough the terrible twins had tremendous respect for big brother, they almost revered him; he seemed to be the one they regarded in high esteem even better than they regarded me, their mother. And so even if he was not around, when he eventually went to boarding school, the terrible twins never entered into big brother's bedroom. Joe was meticulous, he always kept his bedroom neat and tidy all the time, nothing was ever out of place. His most treasured possession in there was his keyboard that he had learnt playing from around the age of 5.

On the other hand, the terrible twins shared a bedroom; they slept on bunk beds with the younger of the two occupying the upper deck. Occasionally the beds were placed side by side but the down side when this happened was they would be talking and laughing and playing for longer than I would have wanted. Because of these differences between Joe and 'them'; it was of no consequence to either party that the terrible twins were going, and Joe was staying behind. For big brother this was even more ideal as this meant less noise in the house; something that he always complained about. It also meant more peace and monopoly especially when it came to watching television!

While my mother was putting together a few clothes in a small case for the boys; the boys came to my bedroom to find me and to ask if I was coming along with them and their uncle? When I told them that I was staying behind because of work, the boys cuddled me one at a time and reassured me; "don't worry, we will come back soon, we are just going to school"; it melted my heart I wanted to cry but I didn't. After taking turns to kiss me on the forehead they both ran out straight to their uncle's car.

It turned out; as I later learnt from the uncle's housemaid who loved me deeply; the main motivator for leaving with uncle appeared to have been going on a car ride. Since their father passed away car rides were now few and far between. I was told that as soon as it was time to go to bed they cried themselves to sleep when the plea to be taken back home to mamma was received with threats of being spanked by their auntie. (This marked a painful turbulent journey for the two boys; particularly Jack; which would last close to a year).

After the boys and their uncle left; before leaving Reverend Ntuli narrated to me how the meeting in the car had gone. He said he had spoken to my brother-in-law and read to him snippets from his small pocket size Bible that he carried with him everywhere. He said he read to him verses on what God says about what happens to people who ill-treat widows and orphans. After reading the Bible and a lengthy discussion Rev had offered to pray for my brother-in-law so he could receive healing from his recent bereavement, after the loss of his brother. He said he had also prayed for my brother-in-law so that he could gain wisdom and guidance from the Lord with which to deal with things and my brother- in- law had humbly accepted the offer. Prayer changes situations all the time when the motive is right and is in sync with God's will.

As soon as everyone had left my mother could not wait to go and check on my son Joe who was still hiding in his bedroom. She had an in-depth discussion with my son and the following day she gave me a blow by blow account of what they had talked about. My son Joe has always been a closed book; he does not wear his heart on his sleeve. Getting him to express his thoughts, emotions and feelings had always been an uphill struggle that requires a great deal of tact.

It was therefore extraordinary that when my mother went in and sat beside Joe and asked him why he had refused to come out and greet his uncle Joe immediately came out of his blankets; sat upright and looked his grandmother straight in the eyes and proceeded to say; "You grandmother I know you still have your father and mother; is that right?" My mother who was blessed to still have both of her parents and was very close to them replied; 'yes I do'. The boy went on to ask; "Are you always happy when you are with your parents?", my mother said she was always very happy; which she was!

My boy then proceeded to say; "Let's say you, grandmother; that your father becomes sick and he dies, and your uncles start to make your mother unhappy and cause her to cry all the time; and they also take your father's car from your mother and your mother is left with nothing, would you want to greet your uncles or go with them to their homes?"

My mother reported that she was caught completely off guard by these scenarios and hard questions; so much so that while she was still trying to figure out the best way to answer these questions; the boy remarked; "You see Grandma, that's why I will never talk to him or go to his house ever again". Grandmother was therefore firmly placed in a more difficulty position; in a tight corner! Even I when I heard this I was quite shocked to hear this. I thought I had been doing a really great job of hiding my pain and suffering from my children; obviously not; the boy had been observing and reading in between the lines because I never talked about what was going on while they were within earshot. This also indicated that the poor child had been deeply traumatised by all the preceding events and had no opportunity to talk to anyone about this until now. Was this not a form of child neglect?

In an attempt to salvage the pathetic situation my mother, a practising woman of faith then reminded my son that his uncles loved him and his brothers very much. She then attempted to point out that whatever problems were between me his mother and his uncles; he was only a child; and that he shouldn't get involved. At this point the boy reportedly told his grandmother; "Well, it is too late now because I am already involved".

At this point my mother reported that she attempted to be firmer with him by categorically telling him that he had no business meddling in the affairs of adults; but this too backfired. She was even more surprised when the boy hit back stating also very firmly; "My mother is my business, anyone who hurts my mother is also hurting me, that is why I told you I am already involved."

Completely lost for words and in complete resignation my mother then calmly asked the boy; "Now that you say all this is your business and that you are already involved; what are you going to do about it since you are just a young small boy and your uncles are all big men?" For the first time the boy had nothing to say; after a brief moment of silence he replied; "I don't know" before sobbing so much the grandmother ended up rocking him on her lap like a baby. He cried for a long time until he was sweating so profusely. That evening when my brother went to call them for dinner, they both declined, and they were both asleep in Joe's bed.

> *And God will wipe away every tear from their eyes; there shall be no more death, no sorrow, no crying. There shall be no more pain, for the former things have passed away. (Revelation 21:4)*

CHAPTER SEVEN

TURBULENT TIMES; AS DEPRESSION SINKS IN

For I know the thoughts I think towards you saith the Lord, thoughts of peace and not evil, to give you an expected end. (Jeremiah 29:11)

The first three months of living in my new place of residence at my work place with my family in fragments was a new way of life that I had to learn and quickly adapt to. This was my new reality now. Of all the challenges that I had gone through, this challenge was not just difficult; it was heart-breaking in equal measure. I quickly noticed that my 2 smaller children were not happy anymore.

My middle boy Jack appeared more affected than his younger brother. When they were dropped off on Fridays they appeared rather withdrawn, very fragile, and portrayed a picture of people who have been hard-done-by and are just grateful to be alive. Their relationship with me changed from a mutual fun, loving relationship to one tainted with ambivalence and mistrust. During the days they were at home with me they abandoned their own bedroom; a place they previously both seemed to relish and take great pleasure in calling their own space. They both started sleeping in my bed with me. The little joy they radiated on Fridays and Saturdays when they were at home tended to gradually fade away come Saturday bedtime as the thoughts of going back to their uncle began to occupy their little minds. Indeed, by Sunday morning they would progressively become more irritable and moody. This also heralded the onset of Jack's tantrums. He also began having nightmares, crying in his sleep and bedwetting; something that he had never done before.

Whenever their uncle or auntie turned up to pick them up on Sunday evenings; they would remain seated quietly looking frightened and confused. The auntie would usually come to the door and call out their names and this would work like magic as the boys would go running to the car and sit at the back seat quietly. Our housemaid or my mother would follow behind with their little satchels containing their books and a few clothes.

It would not be until many years later when he was in his late teens Jack would briefly become a slightly more rebellious and troublesome teenager when he was able to talk about the trauma that he had gone through while being looked after by his uncle and auntie. By this time Jack had developed a fully-fledged love/hate relationship with me. We had regular altercations that seemingly originated from nowhere. One minute he was a wonderful loving teen; cuddling me and buying me expensive jewellery with the little money that he got from his after-school job that he had at the local hotel and would be telling me I was the best mother in the entire world; the next minute he was having tantrums and telling me all sorts. He and his two brothers had just recently joined me in a foreign country and while his two brothers were settling in very well; I just thought Jack was having difficulties adjusting to this life changing experience. Little did I know that this was just a trigger of early childhood trauma.

On this particular day; after so many years in the future post the death of my husband; after a particularly challenging altercation; and I had heard enough; I threatened Jack that if he was not prepared to follow my instruction; I was going to send him back home, to our country of origin. I reminded him how I had fought and shed sweat and tears for him to be allowed into the country; and pointed to him how he was driving me to the point where I was prepared to put in the same effort to have him send back.

At this point Jack would break down emotionally and for the first time he opened up; "I know you want to send me back because you have never loved me; If you really loved me mamma; why did you let my uncle and auntie take me when I was a child? Do you know how much I suffered at their house? Do you know how I was always beaten up and scolded for nothing all the time that I was there? They never loved me mamma. So, you want to send me back to the people who ill-treated when I was only an innocent small child? It was the worst, longest year of my life; I was only a little boy mamma; you did not protect me; you let me down mamma"; It was one of the most difficult things to hear. What made it more difficult to hear was the fact that I had suspected it; but had felt helpless and so was unable to do anything about it.

This would mark the first day that we had both talked about the difficulties that we had during those early years. This day also would mark the beginning of healing and restoration of our fragmented mother/son relationship. Yes; I had failed my son; perhaps I should have at least fought to keep all my children from the very beginning; but what would I have done with their schooling? The nearest school for children their age was three kilometres away, it was not accessible; as there were no transport links between our house and the school. Strangely enough though, while Jack endured the beatings and scolding; his young brother on the other hand appears to have been treated very well and consequently all he remembers is his auntie used to feed him lots of cake; and no scars whatsoever.

Meanwhile, going back to those first three months when his two younger brothers no longer lived at home and were reduced to weekend visitors only; my eldest son Joe; just at that early age; appeared to have suddenly grown up and matured overnight. After refusing to go and have an easy life of not only living closer to his school; but being chauffer driven there every day Joe quickly established his own routine independently.

He would wake up before 5 o'clock every school day to bath, have some porridge and walk the one-mile journey to catch the early commuter bus on his first leg of the journey. Come summer, rain or sunshine, my son never required prompting or encouragement even once; neither did he even complain. He did everything and managed himself just like every mature and responsible adult does; at the age of ten. After leaving home so early in the morning he would be back home around 6 o'clock in the evening. School ended at 4 o'clock in the evening; however, the commute back home was so challenging as it would be rush hour.

There were no school buses but ordinary buses for all passengers and hence usually the people who boarded these buses often had to fight their way into the few buses as they were not able to meet the passenger demands. Hence my small son often had to keep away and let the big men and women fight their way into the early buses first to avoid being injured in the fracas. Joe had always been a quiet and reserved child and these challenges made him even more quiet. There was no doubt that this routine was wearing him down physically and mentally, but Joe always tried as much as he could to portray that all was well. What choice did he have after adamantly declining the offer to go and live at his uncle's house in luxury? From such an early age he was able to demonstrate that he was a man who kept his word through thick and thin.

Watching my three children's once happy lives torn apart and their apparent unhappiness began to take its toll on me. I had no resources with which to support them and make their lives a little easier. There were no suitable schools nearby; within walking distance. I was caught between the proverbial deep blue sea and a hard rock. The situation was very bleak.

This was another very dark phase along the turbulent journey. Before I knew what was going on I found myself sliding helplessly into a bottomless pit of despair. How I managed to remain functional and hold a full time, challenging job that came with enormous responsibility was nothing short of another of God's countless miracles.

Before I knew it, I had got fully embedded into a routine of waking up, attend to my personal hygiene, go to work, come back home in the evening and go straight to my bedroom and sleep. Just like the proverbial walking dead. Sitting in the lounge and watching TV or sitting at the kitchen table for whatever meal all became chores that were simply too much for me to deal with. If I was not at work; 'working'; I was in bed asleep, no matter what day or time it was?

My amazing mother would prepare a tray with food, drinks and fruit and bring it to my bedroom. She would also go out of her way to find and prepare some snacks that she knew I liked such as roast salted peanuts, round nuts etc but my appetite for them appeared to have completely left me. She would wake me up softly and encouraged me to at least try and eat something. She would not leave until she felt I had eaten to her satisfaction. The longer I took to wake up and eat my food the longer she stayed in the room. She soon devised her own plan of coming in with her Bible under her armpit with both of her hands on the food tray. After placing the food on the bedside table and prompting me to wake up and have my food, mum would sit on a chair right opposite me and read her Bible until I finish eating. Eventually, even after I have finished eating my food and she clears everything away; she would come back after the washing up and continue reading her Bible well into midnight. Before leaving she would kneel by my bedside; sing a whole hymn softly and sorrowfully and then give a very long heartfelt prayer then would retire to her own bedroom.

> **The name of the Lord is a strong tower; The righteous runneth into it and is safe. (Proverbs 18:10)**

CHAPTER EIGHT

THE ARRIVAL OF A NEW DAWN

Come unto me all ye that labour and are heavy laden and I will give thee rest. (Matthew 11:20)

This unhealthy pattern of going through the motions and floating in between sleeping and going to work went on for what appeared to have been forever. Well; for five and half months to be precise, how could I ever forget that momentous day?

I heard a very unusual faint knock on my bedroom door. It was unusual because whoever was behind the door was not one of my regular visitors who just knocked once or twice and opened the door before I even respond. I was used to people doing this so much so that I did not even bother with responding. When the knock became slightly louder I raised my voice and encouraged my visitor to come in. I noticed that it was now dark and, so I switched on my bedside lamp. The clock said it was seven in the evening. Joe opened the door and walked towards my bed and with a sombre voice he politely asked me if he could sit on my bed. I beckoned him to come and sit beside me, but he chose to sit opposite me.

He sat opposite me cross- legged, supporting his head by holding his chin with both palms. He sat quietly looking at me. This was not just unusual, it was weird, truly bizarre. Sensing that something was not right, this was no casual visit, I quickly sat up fully and looked at him; waiting for him to say something; anything at all!

As soon as he noticed that I had given him my full attention Joe started softly; "Mamma, what day is it today?". I hesitantly replied; 'It is Saturday son, what's the matter?'.

Yes, I knew it was Saturday because on Saturdays I did not go to work. On Saturdays my routine was quite specific, I woke up around four o'clock in the morning because I will have run out of sleep anyway. The other main motivator was that during this time I did not have to bump into anybody who may have been fully awake. I would have a long bath, put on a fresh dressing gown, have a bowl of cereal and leave a note for my mother not to bring me any breakfast with evidence of this unwashed bowl to allay her fears that I might starve to death in my sleep! Then I would go back straight to bed.

The big idea behind this was to keep myself, my misery and hopelessness tucked safely away and hidden under my blankets; away from everyone, particularly my children. The three boys were all at home as this was school holidays. The two brothers had left my bed earlier in the morning and had never returned; they had been out playing all day with friends of similar age group from the neighbourhood. Today was a Saturday no different from any other, and so I thought.

As soon as I said it was Saturday son; my son went on to ask me even more courteously; "Mamma, what date is it today, what month is this?"

Oh my God! It was at this point that the gravity of the situation hit me in the face; It was his birthday! His tenth birthday! Feeling completely useless, and just as I struggled to find the most appropriate lame excuse to provide; the boy burst out crying, which was also very unusual, and it took me by a huge surprise because under normal circumstances this boy was not just quiet and resilient; he was also defiant. He never cried publicly like he was doing now. Even when his father passed away, I never saw him shed tears in front of me; he would do this behind his firmly shut bedroom door; only his wet, red eyes and sometimes evidence of dry streaks of tears on his cheeks would betray him.

In between sorbs he asked; "Do you know how much I have waited for this day to come; mamma? Do you have any idea how I have longed and counted down to this day? Now it has gone just like that. It came when you were fast asleep in your bed and has gone still with you in your bed asleep; all of it; all gone and finished; just like that; and it will never return; my tenth birthday will never come again. To think that I have even ran down the corridor when I heard your bedroom door open; when you were going to the bathroom; I have even met you along the corridor and tried bumping into you so that you could at least notice my presence and have your memory jogged? You could not even just stop and say to me; 'Happy Birthday Joe'. Did you not see me mamma? All day I have been trying to look for clues and telling myself that may be mamma wants to make my tenth birthday a surprise this year; maybe at supper time everything is going to unfold; supper time has come and gone without you mamma even turning up at the table. Everyone is now just waiting to go to bed. Mamma how could you do that to me?"

He refused to be consoled. In the end I just had to apologise and tell him the truth- that I had simply forgotten that it was his birthday.

On hindsight; I should have just ended there, and not tried to give any rationale or excuse rather! However, because of a desperate need to exonerate myself and come out of this mess relatively clean I attempted to justify my profound loss of memory by explaining that; "I forgot because the past few months have been very hard for me, because my husband just died".

I might as well have poured a gallon of petrol onto roaring flames; I certainly would have achieved the same result! My son's reaction to that statement brought me a huge wakeup call; "And so you forgot about my birthday because your husband died. Is that so mamma? What about me? What about my brothers Jack and Gerald? Did it ever occur to you that I lost my father? I lost my father mamma, just in case you didn't notice. At least you still have your father; do you realise how blessed you are mamma? You still have both of your parents and one full set of grandparents at your age. What about me; I just turned ten today and already have no father; did it ever occur to you that I might need cheering up; especially on my first birthday without my father? Me and Jack and Gerald lost our father; but it's like we lost our mother too. Mamma we still have you at least; we need you to play with us; to watch cartoons with us; to take us for walks and picnics up the mountains like you and dad used to do. We need you to remember our birthdays; they just come once a year mamma. We need you to bake us cakes and sing us happy birthday songs just the way you used to. If you have no money you can at least just hug us and say, 'happy birthday'; it does not cost anything mamma."

This was one of the most effective life changing lectures that I had ever heard. Words of wisdom from a ten-year-old boy that brought me face to face with who I really was. Yes, I was still as selfish and as self-centred just as I was when my husband was still alive.

Throughout my married life my loving, kind and caring husband always used to light-heartedly joke that I should pray to God that if death was to come to our house prematurely I should be the first to go so that our children would not end up destitute and, on the streets, begging for food. He would say this behind closed doors when it was just the two of us; after one of my many shopping sprees. Whenever he said this I would laugh it off but agree with him in a very strange sort of way because I was aware that my biggest shortcoming was an almost pathological, insatiable desire for loads and loads of nice clothes. I was a vain, naïve, and irresponsible spoilt wife when it came to budgets and use of my pay cheque.

As soon as I received my pay cheque I would be off to the local boutiques and major shops on the high street to purchase the latest offering on their 'just arrived' outfit rails; just for myself but with my dear husband in tow as he had to drive me there. I had such a reputation and was quite well known by the boutique owners and sales personnel of these shops, so much that they always had something fancy put aside for me, ready for me to pay for and collect; I was such a joke.

My supportive, dutiful husband would always be with me as at the time I was unable to drive. In His infinite wisdom God only gave me the motivation to learn how to drive and I got my driver's licence exactly twelve months before my husband passed away.

While David made light of my reckless spending on just myself and commented that I ought to ask God that He should take me first; however, when other people such as his family tried to say anything negative about me and my obscenely extravagant wardrobe my husband would always jump to my defence. He would say something so wonderfully amazing such as; "My wife has a very difficult job, she works very hard, she deserves all her nice clothes. If having many nice clothes is what makes her happy; why not? If she is happy; I her husband am happy because that's what our relationship is all about".

It would not be until soon after he was late; how on reflection these sorts of altercations may have played a part in the way that I then got treated after he was no longer there to protect me. He was always supporting and defending me whenever criticism, with or without base was levelled against me.

Since my own income was spent selfishly and lavishly on myself; my poor husband's income paid for all our household expenses; every bill, food, transportation, children's requirements etcetera. He never pointed out that I was selfish and self-centred, not even on a single day.

…..."me and Jack and Gerald lost our father mamma; but it's like we have lost our mother too"; those words pierced like a double-edged sword. Ever since my husband passed away; I had preserved myself by sleeping through my bereavement and challenges and neglected my children in the process. My son's words were like a bulb that has just been lit in a once very dark room. Yes, I was hopelessly failing my children as I wallowed and was consumed by my own misery, grief and self-pity. I had to wake up and rise to the occasion. I had to change my whole attitude and perspective. I was letting down my children and it had to stop and stop now.

I however needed a lot of grace for me to creep out of this garbage dump successfully. I had to get out, there was no way I was going to carry on like this. What was worse? During the last four months I had almost doubled in weight; with my dress size jumping from a petit size twelve to size eighteen!

That night I went down on my knees and stayed there longer than I have ever done as I begged and pleaded for forgiveness; strength and wisdom so I could be a better mother to my wonderful children. For the first time since my husband passed away I began to see the many countless blessings that surrounded me! I was not a victim anymore. I was blessed, and I was going to rise up and behave like the blessed one! I began to join my mother during her daily Bible reading sessions; and also joined her especially during the bedtime prayers. My relationship and intimacy with the Lord was completely enhanced and began to grow from strength to strength.

> *The Lord is nigh unto them that are of a broken heart;*
> *and saveth such as be of a contrite spirit. (Psalm 34:18)*

CHAPTER NINE

GOD REALLY WORKS IN MYSTERIOUS WAYS!

Fear thou not; for I am with thee: be not dismayed; for I am thy God: I will strengthen thee; yea, I will uphold thee with the right hand of my righteousness: (Isaiah 41:10)

Through the grace of God, by the time that my mother left to go back to her own home my spiritual life had been completely transformed. What was more amazing was how transformation in just this one aspect of my life triggered a domino effect in every other area of my life. Suddenly, I had no space in my life's diary for just sleeping outside night-time sleeping hours! Not only that; the more active I became, the faster my weight began to shed off. I had a full active life and routine that I loved and looked forward to on all days of the week once again; this was amazing!

Our church attendance and participation in all major church activities became a major part of our daily lives. At home we began to sing hymns and read our bibles together as a family every evening before we went to bed. I bought my three sons age appropriate Bibles; the two younger boys' Bibles were more colourful with lots of pictures and cartoons;

when they went to their uncle's, they often carried these Bibles in their little satchels.

At church I also joined the church choir. This meant that I had to go to church in the evenings from Thursday to Saturday for choir practice in preparation for the Sunday service and other occasional choir competitions. I also started volunteering my time, services and substance to some of the church activities such as feeding the hungry and homeless.

The more I got involved in all these activities the better I began to feel within myself. I began to regain and experience unspeakable peace and joy right in the midst of my storms. The force and impact of these storms on me began to become weaker and weaker and appeared to fade off into oblivion; and got replaced instead by my new package of peace and joy.

I had so much energy; I was now almost always on the go. I now even had time to visit my two younger boys after work and got to spend an hour or so with them every other week day. After meeting with the younger boys, I would proceed to go and meet with my eldest son at a prearranged place and together we would travel home. Spending half of my life asleep was no longer my portion; I had so much to keep me awake and live for!

Whenever my three children were at home for the weekend or during school holidays, we would do everything together; from housework, cooking, baking, watching videos and going for walks. I also began to take them with me to all my church activities whenever they were not at school.

I remember taking the boys to watch a Christian theatrical drama by an evangelist from abroad that was organized by our local church. It was about how believers in Jesus Christ will go to paradise and how none believers will end up in the lake of fire. It was quite a captivating drama with a real message. At the end of the drama the evangelist invited all those who wanted to receive Jesus Christ as their personal Lord and Saviour into their lives to come in front and was quite touched that all my three young sons ran to the pulpit.

The closer I began to walk with the Lord; the more my eyes were opened to the tremendous suffering all around me. My heart appeared to have suddenly become incredibly more sensitive and fragile as I began to notice the blind woman sitting by the supermarket entrance holding a crying baby and another child holding a little bowl with a few pennies in it; the dishevelled elderly gentleman sitting by the roadside covering himself with an old blanket etc.

Now and again I began to see myself impulsively give away my bag of groceries to the woman and her children; buy a blanket and hand it over to the man by the roadside; and I even began to give away my clothes to the odd woman at church who looked like her situation was worse than mine. Eventually I turned what initially started as random acts of kindness into a new way of life; habits that I did when I got my pay cheque. I even remembered that odd family in my past as well as present neighbourhood who would benefit from a bag of the staple food; mealie meal, a bottle of cooking oil or a packet of sugar and would buy this and deliver these to them. Despite this and with only one pay cheque we never lacked nor went to bed hungry even for a single day.

Yes; the more I shifted my focus from me and my problems and refocused my attention, energy and substance onto my more disadvantaged neighbours the more fulfilled and rich I became spiritually and even materially. My hunger for new clothes died a natural death as I became aware I had too many. The great joy and sense of freedom that I experienced from simply creating small packages and giving them away was amazing. I had been in bondage, experiencing fake joy from my piles of clothes and had not been even aware. This liberation was quite exhilarating! During this time there was also a catastrophic hurricane and floods in the neighbouring country and I felt quite privileged I was able to send several boxes of clothes; including all of my late husband's clothes.

I began to see how blessed and privileged I was every single day that I woke up and felt overwhelmed and humbled by God's amazing grace. I had been blind but now I could see! I had absolutely nothing to whinge about. Instead of feeling sorry for myself and my children I began to have an attitude of gratitude because my blessings were countless. I simply could not count them all even if I tried. Day and night, I began to meditate on God's goodness, mercy and kindness towards me and my children and I could not praise the Lord enough.

Within about ten months of abandoning my victim mentality and adopting a completely new way of life; through God's amazing grace; everything around me and my children also began to change in very mysterious ways.

The first thing that happened was that my brother-in-law and his wife's financial circumstances took a very big crash; so much so that they even lost the very house they were living in. As a result, they could no longer afford to look after my children as well as their own. This meant that after eleven turbulent months my two sons were now back home with me and their bigger brother for good. My late husband's vehicle was also returned a week or so before my children were brought back. At the time the boys were returned a new pre-school for young children was opened just ten minutes' walk away from our house and a few children from the neighbourhood had just started going there. As the school was still new, they were still enrolling new pupils and it was not difficult getting the boys into this school.

While Jack remained slightly less trusting of me and would throw a tantrum now and again; however, within several weeks he completely stopped bedwetting, crying in his sleep and having nightmares also ceased. All my children looked generally very happy again and they were all growing into very nice, responsible and ambitious little people.

They all worked very hard at whatever they did, and their names were never missing from the prize giving lists at their respective schools! God was really; really turning things around and steering us all in a different direction!

It was just so wonderful to have my children all under one roof and for them to come and open the door for me whenever I got home from work. Indeed, the Lord fought this battle for me yet again; I did not have to say anything. Our God is indeed able to do all things for us if we let him and if we align ourselves in accordance with his will for our lives. Through this occurrence that I never ever envisaged I learnt to trust and to depend on him more and more.

By the time my two younger boys started primary school, their brother was now in high school at one of the best boarding schools in the country. The two boys found places at a very good primary school in town; however, going there was no longer a problem as I now had access to a company vehicle. Their father's car had just been brought back however, the car had to be towed to my house because it now needed a complete engine overhaul and I did not have the sort of money required for such a big job.

A few months after the car and my boys were at home; one evening the boys handed to me a thick brown envelope that they said had been brought to the house by someone they had never seen while I was in my bedroom. The stranger had declined to stay when informed I was in the bedroom, and that I can come to meet with him. Inside the big envelope was a Christmas card; yes, this was the last week of November, Christmas was around the corner. To my utter disbelief; inside the Christmas card was a thick wad of new crisp dollars and after counting them they amounted to five times my monthly salary; my salary for almost half a year!

Desperate to know if this was a mistake I read the Christmas card again and sure enough it was for me; this stranger had also done his homework, he had spelt my children's names very well. He had simply written; "This is for you, so you can give your children a very wonderful Christmas this year!" There was no name or signature, never recognized the handwriting, never knew who left the envelope and never knew who to ask.

The company that I worked for was church- related; it was frequented by many great God-fearing visitors from abroad. I had heard a few similar stories from workmates who had such encounters and so that information helped me to remain grounded. Even if I did not know who had been so kind and generous towards me and my children, I did know that this was God, yet again working in mysterious ways. He had impressed upon someone's heart to bless us with this unwarranted, unearned, unsolicited and indeed undeserved gift! It was not just enough to give the boys a Christmas of a lifetime, it was also enough to put our vehicle back on the road, to pay off all my debts and indeed to pay the boys' fees for a whole year. My God was at work, manifesting in many weird and wonderful ways in our lives. He provided for all needs even those I thought were too big to even think about; how amazing and awesome was the Lord! If this was not the Lord, whose doing was this? My faith in him could no longer be shaken!

It would not be until around January of the following year when one of the many frequent visitors to the institution passed by my office and after the usual greetings he enquired specifically about what type of Christmas my children had that my curiosity was reignited. I suspected that he was our kind and generous benefactor. Just as he was about to walk out through the door my curiosity got the better of me; I could not help it and I quickly blatantly asked; 'Excuse me please, before you go I have a very odd question to ask; did you by any chance leave a large brown envelope with a Christmas card and something else at my house in November?'

He attempted to pretend he did not know what I was talking about but in the end, he painstakingly tried to explain how he had no hidden agenda; in fact, he had fought very hard against giving me the money because he needed it himself!

I invited him back and begged him to tell me the whole story. After taking a seat, he was able to tell me exactly how much was in the envelope. He said that he had received the whole amount as compensation for his lost luggage. He narrated how as soon as he received the money he kept being prompted by a voice from deep within his spirit to give the whole amount 'to that lady and her children who live in that particular house'. My whole heart started pounding as he narrated his story. He said he struggled with this voice and felt a huge burden as he tried to resist the voice and keep the money. He said for three days he had no peace day and night until the minute he came and left the entire envelope and its contents with my children with instructions to give it to me.

He also explained another very strange phenomenon. He said as soon as he left the envelope at my house the following morning after handing over his compensation money for his lost very expensive luggage, that had been missing for just over ten days, and hence the compensation money had just been received; the airline called him to let him know that his lost luggage had been found in one of the cities that he had passed through. He was also told the luggage would be delivered to him before the evening and that he could also keep his compensation money as a gesture of good will and for the inconvenience of going without his luggage for that long. His luggage had subsequently arrived that same day, as promised. At the end he laughed everything off and said; "God just wanted my airline to give you that money; it was not my money; I did not work for it; well, I just went for about two weeks without my creature comforts and I did just fine"! It was the most amazing, extraordinary story that I have ever heard in all my life; and I was not just a part of it; I was at the centre of this amazing story! My God was real, working behind the scenes in mysterious ways for my good!

And ye shall seek me and find me, when ye shall search for me with all your heart. (Jeremiah 29:13)

65

CHAPTER TEN

TRUSTING GOD THROUGH THE STORMS

Looking unto Jesus the author and finisher of our faith; who for the joy that was set before Him endured the cross, despising the shame, and is sat down at the right hand of the throne of God. (Hebrews 12:2)

During the months that my mother stayed with us, taking care of us; I kept overhearing her lamenting and making the same statement repeatedly whenever her friends, sisters or her own mother came to check on how we were all doing after our tragic loss.

My mother would always start the conversation by thanking and acknowledging how God was sustaining us; but she would then look around to see how close or far away I was from her so that she could adjust the volume and tone of her voice accordingly. It was evident to me that she did not want me to hear whatever she was going to say next and this made me even more inquisitive as I highly suspected the talk was about me.

After scanning her environment she would take a deep breath, with a noticeable deep in her mood and would proceed; 'Well, what can I do; It's just that my daughter is too young to be a widow; if only this could have happened to me and not her; (not sure how happy my father would have been hearing that kind of statement coming from his wife!); it gives me sleepless nights sometimes to think that at such a young age she has to carry the burden of being a widow". The first time I heard her say that; while it grabbed my attention, I quickly dismissed it as just small talk.

However, when I heard her make the same comments to different relatives and friends for the second and third time I began to reflect on what her exact fears were? I knew for certain that she was a very loving and overprotective mother; I also thought of myself as a very seasoned, confident and competent woman. I had a decent job and a place I now called home; what was she talking about? What an odd thing to say that, 'I was too young to carry the burden of being a widow?' I really did not understand her fears at all, initially that is.

On the day that my wonderful mother eventually left to go back home, to my father; about six months after my husband's death I tried to take this opportunity to reassure her that I was going to do just fine as she had helped me so much through the critical times.

I explained to her that I was now in a much better place; and that she should not continue to have sleepless nights as this was not good for her health. I could see my mother's eyes welling up with tears as she tried to hide that away from me by quickly hugging me and burying her face behind my shoulder; while she nodded in agreement with what I was saying to her, she did not say anything verbally. In a way I was left a little deflated by her apparent lack of confidence in my strength and abilities that I myself rated as a lot higher than average.

However, as months became years; and just one and half years along the road post my husband's death, I began to feel the real burden of widowhood as it became apparent and began to take its toll on me. It was only then that I began to understand what my mother's fears were all about. Very strange, how could she have known? She had never experienced widowhood herself before; neither were any of her many sisters; and even her own mother still had my grandfather!

Being a young widow with three small children just starting school can be extremely challenging; I did not escape any of the challenges. It comes with a wide range of many other complex problems; the list is endless.

At a much deeper and personal level there is a peculiar type of loneliness and longing for companionship with someone of the opposite sex, which really have nothing to do with the physical act, well, in most cases that is! Even just the reality that; that man is permanently no longer there to listen to you moan about your boss or the difficult or wonderful day that you have had at work begins to weigh heavily on your mood and sense of well-being. How married women often take their blessing of having a husband for granted! Strange as it may sound; you begin to sadly miss even the absence of his pyjamas and dirty socks carelessly discarded on the bathroom floor right next to the empty washing basket; something that used to make you hit the roof with rage and anger! Some advice to all the wives out there who do not appreciate their husbands very much; "Cherish him with care, for you will never know the heartache until you see his empty chair", someone once said.

On the other end of the spectrum is the day to day routine of juggling work, running a home, children's school activities, social activities and the twenty-four hours full time job of parenting three overactive boys who are still growing up. Supporting three children through attendance at all school activities on its own can be a logistical nightmare as certain important school activities may clash with important meetings at work. It becomes even more complicated, particularly when the children go to different schools and they are still young; the last thing you want to do is to let them down by not showing up on their special day.

Support from family members or friends with attendance at their school's special day on your behalf does not always fly well either; especially with underage children as I quickly learnt. On a particular consultation day; (a day when parents visit the school to look at their children's books and have a meeting with the class teacher); this took place while I was at a week-long conference out of town. The class teacher later told me that as soon as my sister-in-law walked in to look at Gerald's books, he quickly grabbed his books away from his auntie and cried; 'she is not my real mother; my real mother will come and see them next week, she told me she will be coming back next week'. It was slightly awkward and embarrassing for both my sister-in-law and for the teacher; however, in the end the teacher had to bargain with the boy so that his auntie could look at his books. On my return the teacher had to honour her side of the bargain by giving me special permission to go in on a particular day to look at the books again and consult with her about Gerald's performance. This eventually worked out well.

Juggling all these unaided can also sometimes be enough to cause any woman a nervous breakdown. The pressure may cause one to lose all sense of direction through constantly running around playing catch up as well as trying to catch one's breath in a very literal sense.

Even with God on my side there were many times that I felt lost and completely overwhelmed by my circumstances so much so that I wondered how long I was going to last; more so since I was living in a society that appeared to turn a blind eye to my 'new group' of social class. Socially and even in church there were several fun activities for various categories of people such as 'the couples evening; the singles retreats, etc'; but none for widows. Even though now single; a retreat or forum for singles made up of eighteen to thirty-year-old spinsters looking for romance and possibly a life partner was hardly a place for a thirty- something old mother of three to fit in. On the other hand, even if there were to be 'a widows' group', how many widows would have been in my local small church? And if for argument's sake there were four or five other widows; what were the chances that any of them would have been below age fifty? Zero to nil was more likely to be the range. This was a sad, no win situation.

I also soon discovered that as a young widow I was in a very vulnerable position. I soon found myself being a target of all sorts of weird and wonderful men, most of whom were married. Some of them were so weird so much so that they even had the guts to try and get my attention through forming dubious relationships with my innocent little children. Buying them little presents, offering them rides in their fancy cars whenever they met them along the way and even coming to request to take them out to movies on the odd day during school holidays. Some would also go as far as arranging to pick them up and taking them to Wimpy (a fast food outlet); all these became bait with which to catch me their mother.

Incidentally this was a small close-knit community where no one was a stranger; offering rides to small children was considered safe; in fact, it was viewed quite positively; as acts of kindness. This was therefore encouraged and considered normal. Initially this set up was quite challenging indeed. Depending on what other challenges were running concurrently, with all the best intentions and a desire to keep running sometimes I stumbled.

Coincidentally this was also all happening at a time when the local television station was screening a lot of locally produced dramas in the local language, highlighting the rising massive social problem of child abuse mostly in blended families were young children were often physically, emotionally and psychologically traumatised by their step parent.

One day as we were all sitting at the kitchen table having breakfast, a visiting auntie of mine, my mother's young sister gave the boys compliments for behaving well demonstrated by their listening to me their mother and obeying my instructions. The boys appeared to take great pleasure in being given this positive feedback. As they sat there pouring their tea and coffee, making toast while relishing and savouring the compliments; completely from the blue my auntie changed the subject and completely destroyed the lovely breakfast experience. Simultaneously she also undid the effect of the positive feedback that she had given earlier.

Perhaps thinking that she was being helpful and doing me a favour my auntie went on to ask the boys; "Are you all going to continue to behave so well when your mother gets married again to another man?" They all looked at me, appearing completely shocked; they gave me a quizzical look with the impression that I had lied or cheated them in some way by possibly withholding crucial information from them. I did not like what my auntie had said at all, and I was also shocked and lost for words. Without reading the atmosphere accurately my auntie proceeded to say; "Why are you all looking at me like that? Your mother is free to get married again if she wants; she can have other children too; do you not want her to be married again, do you not want her to be happy again?

Joe my eldest son immediately poured the entire contents of his cup in the sink; threw his slices of toast in the bin and before walking away to the sanctuary of his bedroom he remarked; "I didn't know that my mother was not happy, but if she gets married again I will go and live on the street". The other two younger boys had a slightly different approach to what had been said and all they wanted to know immediately was, when was I going to get married? As soon as I told them that I was not going to get married, this seemed to settle their minds. I am not even sure they understood this message or that it bothered them at all; what appeared to have bothered them more than anything else was their older brother's reaction. They loved him so much that they idolized him; even though he was just about six years older than the middle boy; he was their hero, they all aspired to become like him one day. Especially the way he used to play his keyboard in his bedroom! Seeing him upset affected them quite profoundly and hence even though they resumed to have their breakfast, they were both very quiet.

After breakfast I proceeded to my big boy's bedroom and observed that it was locked, and the key was left in the key hole. After knocking and pleading with him, Joe finally came and opened the door before jumping back into his bed and covering himself from head to toe, evidently still trying to get away from me!

I explained to Joe that I was really upset by what my auntie had said because I had never thought of or talked to anyone about wanting to get married. I told him that I was just so happy because I had him and his two little brothers to make me happy. As soon as I said that Joe threw his blankets away and sat up. We had a long heart to heart conversation and this is when he opened up and I soon realised that he had been watching too many child abuse movies. The child abuse that he saw on TV was in reality affecting him in a very significant way. After having this frank discussion with my son, he made me promise that I was not going to get married while he and his brothers were still young and going to school. I made the promise to my boy that I definitely was not going to.

It was at that point that I made my other life changing, deliberate and conscious decision that I would never bring any man-friend into my home neither would I get married before all my three children had finished university and were working for themselves. My children were aged just under four, six and twelve at the time. I had a very long way to go indeed!

This part of the journey was even more treacherous. There was no way I was going to walk this journey on my own. I needed strength, guidance and wisdom from the Lord God of infinity mercy and wisdom on a day to day basis; hour by hour, minute by minute basis. I needed all the help that the All Knowing Almighty God only could provide. It was tough, it was hard, and it was slippery; at times so slippery so much so that occasionally I would stumble and fall. These occasional pitfalls would always be succeeded by feelings of shame, self-condemnation and despair. However, the good Lord never left or gave up on me; he kept on picking me up, dusting me over and urging me on.

I remember on one of these occasional moments of self-condemnation and despair when I was almost five years into my widowhood; it was on a Monday morning when a male work colleague walked into my office and gave me some startling news. He said that just over the weekend he had attended a bachelor's or stag party. He said at some point during the party talk turned to how each one would feel if he were to die and his beloved wife would go around sleeping with other men. He told me how the discussion turned to how impossible it would be for any young man or woman to just focus on raising his or her children after the death of her spouse. He said at this point; one of the guys said; 'Yes, it is very difficult, but I know of just one young widow who I always meet with her three children in tow every time that I meet her; her husband died about five years ago and I meet her at least once a week; during the whole time I have never ever seen her with any man or heard anything bad said about her.' What my colleague said next is what startled me and touched my heart, I shed a few tears; he said as soon as the guy gave this description, one by one the entire room said they knew exactly the woman the guy was talking about, that she had three little sons; where she worked, and a few mentioned the late husband's name; and that woman was ME!

He concluded by saying how everyone in that room said my late husband was very lucky because 'it is now very rare to find a woman of substance; who has dignity and self-respect like you'. Before he left he said that if his wife turns out to be half the woman that I was, he would be so happy because at least he will have the reassurance that his children will be well looked after. If your late husband is watching he must be really proud of you and is resting in peace"; he concluded.

While deep down I was touched by this unexpected feedback, I brushed off these compliments by saying that I tried my best as my children were now the reason for my life; they were my life.

This was truly a word in season; the best thing that I had ever heard being spoken about me and I felt truly humbled and privileged. It changed the way I kicked and judged myself. I was so encouraged. To me this was God making His presence manifest right on time; at a dark hour, yet again! Perhaps I had been judging myself a little too harshly and God had sent this man to tell me I was doing a great job. The more I focused on God's goodness and love for me the less I stumbled and was able to overcome temptation; the devil and his antics.

Being a widow also comes with other more intricate challenges. As the only surviving parent so early on in your children's lives; your children's vulnerabilities are a little more magnified and somewhat exaggerated. Their dependency on you is almost completely absolute to the point that in an effort to be the best parent that one can be; there is always the danger of overprotecting these children with future diverse adverse consequences.

However, the grimmest of these problems is how; through losing your spouse you are automatically thrown into a position where you begin to think about your own mortality on a very regular basis. Your spouses' recent death brings everything into perspective. It drives home the message of mortality; your very own mortality quite effortlessly and effectively. Unlike before when your spouse was still alive; the possibility of you dying tomorrow becomes real as 'the death folder' moves from the back of your sub-conscious files, right to the forefront of one's conscious mind. Every slight headache begins to present as the initial symptom of that brain tumour that is going to take you, a slight cough becomes the first symptom of lung cancer, the list is endless. Hand in hand with this, is the constant preoccupation with how your vulnerable little children are going to cope when you are gone; who is going to love them and take care of them the way you do? This is always the hardest bit. The incessant preoccupation with dying 'tomorrow' brings with it the perpetual bargaining with God for more time 'to look after my children'. For any normal parent there is no stronger motivation for wanting to live than just the opportunity to take care of one's children.

As a young widow with three young children I did not by-pass any of the above. I soon became aware that there is nothing more spiritual than life and death. I too began to have regular conversations, bargaining with God for more time here on earth so that I could have the chance to raise my children 'to at least a certain age'. For some very strange reason, the bargaining was never for any long-term periods like several years; initially it would always be; 'Please Lord help me to see my children for at least another year;' and would fantasise about how old each one of them would have grown and what things they would be able to do for themselves by the end of that year. At the end of every day and indeed at the end of every year I would feel real gratitude as I learnt not to take anything that I had for granted anymore. The end of the year would also be another tremendous landmark to usher in and yet another bargaining process for the opportunity to see my children into this grade and that grade. How amazing is God's grace and kindness!

Indeed; as I look back now more than twenty-two years after the passing on of my dear husband, I do not see any wickedness in the way that I was treated by my relatives back then. I just see a very loving and caring family that reacted to the tragedy of losing a wonderful brother in an unorthodox way. A way which became the means and vehicle by which I and my children were transported safely and expediently into God's open arms were grace, mercy, favours and miracles that now defines our lives, and who we are resides.

When I look back, I see no darkness anywhere; just blazing light and sunshine. I see the God of complete restoration as my relationship with my relatives is now even better than when my husband walked on earth; we are no longer relatives; we are now proper brothers and sisters who love and care about each other very deeply.

As I reflect on times gone by, I remember not, nor do I see any struggles, pain or suffering, I only see God's righteousness, grace and kindness upon me and my children. When I look at my three children; all grown up, in great health, having worked hard at some of the best universities in a first world country and I paid not a penny; and they are all now highly respected professionals in their chosen fields and, yet they have all remained so obedient, humble, and respectful towards me and everyone they engage with; I see God's amazing and blazing glory.

I see God's faithfulness to all his promises. This should be a source of encouragement especially to all the widows and orphans out there and indeed to anyone who is going through difficulties. If we dare keep our eyes firmly fixed on the cross of Calvary and remain steadfast in our standing on his every promise our tears of distress will turn into tears of joy.

While parts of the journey were brutally painful; I felt God's Omnipresence and his Omnipotence at every stage. I experienced first-hand that God on the mountains is still God in the valleys. If we are destined for the top of the mountain, where glory resides; we have to pass through the deep and sometimes slippery slopes that are at the bottom of the mountain. Flying to the top is discouraged; it robs from us the opportunity to learn and develop into the fullness of who the Lord has called us to be. It is only through the death of Jesus Christ at the cross coupled with living out our daily lives in obedience and to the fullness of who God has called us out to be that will enable us to inherit the crown of glory!

> *Blessed is the one who perseveres under trial because, having stood the test, that person will receive the crown of life that The Lord has promised to those who love him. (James 1:12)*

> *I pray that through reading this book you have been encouraged and blessed. May your relationship with the Lord continue to grow from strength to strength.*

Please look out for my next book: A Life of Miracles; Experiencing God's goodness in a world full of darkness and disorder.

Now unto him that is able to do exceeding abundantly above all that we ask or think, according to the power that worketh in us, unto him be glory in the church by Christ Jesus throughout the ages, world without end. Amen. (Ephesians 3:20-21)

Lightning Source UK Ltd.
Milton Keynes UK
UKHW04f2307160718
325789UK00001B/19/P